THE SOCIAL AUDIT CONSUMER HANDBOOK

THE SOCIAL AUDIT CONSUMER HANDBOOK

A GUIDE TO THE SOCIAL RESPONSIBILITIES OF BUSINESS TO THE CONSUMER

CHARLES MEDAWAR

First published 1978 by
THE MACMILLAN PRESS LTD
London and Basingstoke
Associated companies in New York
Dublin Melbourne Johannesburg and Madras

Typeset, printed and bound
in Great Britain by
REDWOOD BURN LIMITED
Trowbridge & Esher

British Library Cataloguing in Publication Data

Medawar, Charles
    Social audit consumer handbook
    1. Business enterprises—Social aspects
    I. Title
    658.4′08   HD60

    ISBN 0–333–21665–2
    ISBN 0–333–21666–0   Pbk

Public Interest Research Centre Ltd and Social Audit Ltd

Social Audit Ltd is an independent, non-profit-making organisation concerned with improving government and corporate responsiveness to the public generally. Its concern applies to all corporations and to any government, whatever its politics.

Social Audit Ltd is also the publishing arm of *Public Interest Research Centre Ltd*, a registered charity which conducts research into government and corporate activities.

These two organisations are funded mainly by grants and donations and through the sale of publications. Their work has been supported mainly by the Joseph Rowntree Social Service and Charitable Trusts. In addition, support for individual projects has been received from The Social Science Research Council, The Ford Foundation, Consumers' Association, The Allen Lane Foundation, The Elmgrant Trust and other individuals and institutions.

The name *Social Audit* derives by analogy: if there are financial audits—regular reports on the way a company performs its duty to shareholders—why should there not be 'social audits'—reports for employees, consumers, indeed for everyone affected by what a company does?

But *Social Audit* is not only concerned about companies; it believes that democracy is debased by lack of accountability in government and in any other major centre of power. *Social Audit* argues that people must be allowed to know about the decision-making done in their name—and must then be allowed to play the utmost part in controlling their own lives.

Between 1973 and 1976, our reports were published in the journal *Social Audit* which was made available only to subscribers. Reports are now published on a one-off basis and made generally available.

Each issue of the journal *Social Audit* contains three reports—or their equivalent—and each report runs from about 5000 to 10 000 words in length. For details, see pages 144 to 148.

If you would like to place an order or receive further information, please write to **Social Audit Ltd, 9 Poland Street, London W1V 3DG, England.**

Contents

Preface

Our critics will say it, so we will say it first: this book is biased.

It starts from the principle that, in a democracy, decision-makers should account for the use of their power—and that their power should be used as far as possible with the consent and understanding of all concerned.

This book assumes that we should all be concerned, and that we should all want to know what goes on in business and other centres of power. It also assumes that we still are not told much of what we need to know if we are to understand business—as we must, if we are to play a sensible and constructive part in making our society what it might be.

The book is biased about that too. It takes for granted the reader's concern for much of what passes for business—and for much of what is done by those in power, whatever their organisation, creed or political colour. The reader is also expected to believe firmly that it is worth trying to make this and other parts of the world a better place, not least because it might then become one.

But the book is no tract. Working from such assumptions, it tries to set out and explain without undue prejudice why business should account to consumers (among others) and how it might do so far better than it now does.

It does not really do so now, at all. As businesses get fewer and larger —making even some governments seem puny by comparison in power and size—they keep back more and more of the information we need to have about what they really do. They tell us *who* they are, and spend vast sums in doing so. They saturate the air with misinformation as they tell us how wonderful they—as themselves, or as embodied in their products—really are.

In fact, we know very little about the realities of business and— according to many businessmen questioned on this point—might not be at all reassured if we did.[1]

Reassurance is good when you can get it, but facts come first. This book provides facts for consumers about what business is—and about what it does in their name and at their expense. It does this in the style of a 'social audit'. This is an imaginary format (but we think a feasible and desirable one) for presenting the accounts of a company to show not what cash it spent or earned for itsef—but what, in social terms, it cost or gave to the community.

Royalties from the sale of this book will be paid to *Public Interest Research Centre Ltd* (see page v) to further the research and related work that is prompted by such concerns.

January 1978   CHARLES MEDAWAR

Acknowledgement

Public Interest Research Centre Ltd gratefully acknowledges the grant given by *The Ford Foundation* for the research for this book.

Acknowledgement and thanks for their continuing support are due also to the *Joseph Rowntree Charitable* and *Social Service Trusts*, the *Elmgrant Trust*—and to other individual friends.

The author personally acknowledges, with many thanks, the generous help and advice given by the Directors of *PIRC*: Christopher Zealley (Chairman), Andrew Phillips and Oliver Thorold—and by Maurice Frankel and Angela Kaye, on the staff.

To Caroline — for the usual reasons
and many others besides

Part One—
Accounting for Power

1 Power and Responsibility in Business

Underlying issues

Business has power to direct considerable human and other resources on behalf of society. It has far-reaching influence over the way people live, and over the way their societies are run.

A business may use its power wisely and well, or indifferently, or with disastrous effects. As Dahl[1] puts it, a major business corporation may be responsible for death, injury or disease (for example through poor product design or quality control, or through lack of plant safety or excessive pollution). It may deprive people of their livelihood, wellbeing or effective personal freedom (through decision-making on hiring and firing, discrimination, investment or plant location). A major corporation may also influence, control and even coerce individuals or groups, and sometimes nations (for example by manipulating rewards and expectations of rewards and deprivations; by advertising, promotions and propaganda; and by a wide variety of borderline or more patently illegal business practices).

Not surprisingly, the majority of corporations regard the way in which they operate as wholly responsible, both to consumers and to society at large. Indeed, virtually any government, trade union, political party or other major organisation will have the same perceived view of its own propriety—and can always be counted on to provide such evidence of its activities as will support these claims.

If this is natural, it should be natural also to be as deeply suspicious as it is healthy to be about the significance of these claims—if only because there is so little to distinguish them in content, and because they are universally made.

What matters is what an organisation actually does with its power. This will depend on the kind of organisation it is, on what its objects and priorities are, and on the kind of people who run it. It will depend also on what the organisation knows, and cares to find out, about the effects and side-effects of its decisions. And it will depend on what

3

people outside the organisation know and think about what it does—
and on their ability to influence what goes on.

Naturally, an organisation will prefer to avoid any outside interference which may distract it from its chosen course or purpose.
Hence the universal tendency for organisations to exercise private
power—the worst symptoms of which include the growth and tangle of
bureaucracy; the anonymity of officials with decision-making power;
gross public relations machinery; and house rules and disciplines to
encourage and enforce a high degree of secrecy.

There are a few exceptions to be made—but these are exceptions to
a general rule, that secrecy works to the consistent disadvantage of
those outside an organisation, who are affected by what it does. As
another general rule, it may be said that the licence assumed by
decision-makers to use private power to public effect should be
unacceptable on grounds of both practice and principle.

In practice, if the powers of an organisation are not checked at
least enough to prevent or detect abuse, then abuse will occur. And
when abuse does occur—when decisions which may have far-reaching
effects on the daily lives of ordinary people are *not* justified—then they
deserve the close public (or independent) examination that is needed
to put wrongs right. On the other hand, when decisions can be justified,
there would seem generally to be no good reason why they should not
be *publicly* justified—and there are many good reasons why they should.
The main reason—self-evident as a democratic ideal—is to ensure that
power of all kinds is exercised to the greatest possible extent with the
understanding and consent of the public.

Accountability and Business

It is one thing to say there should be full accountability—to say that
those within corporate bodies with decision-making powers should
propose, explain and justify the use of those powers to those without.
It is another thing to suggest how this might be achieved.

The use of a 'social audit' is one possible way. It is neither a straightforward, nor a complete solution: at best it is only a means to the end
of real industrial democracy. The means is an arrangement whereby
business at least systematically answers for its actions to those affected
by what it does.

In the present relationship between business and the community,
this question of accountability does not often arise. When it does, the
traditional response from business is that, within legal limits, the
purpose and practice of business are self-justifying; that business owes
society little or nothing more than it provides by its very existence.

This view is evident in the following remarks made by the then chairman of the largest private corporation in the world, General Motors:

> We have to teach the public, and especially our younger generation, truths which we believe so obvious that they hardly need explanation: that wages for workers, taxes for government, dividends for owners, contributions to education, investment in product improvement, expansion and more jobs—all of these benefits of business to society depend ultimately and entirely on profitability; that profitability and responsibility are inseparable. [2]

Such accounts of business will not do. This one simply enumerates a number of benefits which may be associated with business activity— while it overlooks entirely a wide variety of costs. It also claims an equivalence between profitability and responsibility on the basis of the very proposition it sets out to prove: that profit is in fact wealth for society.

But this is far from established. Many of the costs involved in generating corporate wealth are borne by society and not by the corporation, and in circumstances where it is largely left to the corporation to decide both on the allocation of these costs and on the distribution of the wealth.

It is true that society has, by law and by other means, some control over the distribution of a corporation's surplus wealth; and that attempts are increasingly made to limit and offset the costs incurred in making it. Yet the degree of control is limited. Business is unquestionably permitted on terms which suit business more than anyone else.

Should we not therefore question the right to, and the use of, power in business in something like the following terms: 'Why should citizens, through their government, grant special rights, powers, privileges and protections to any firm, except on the understanding that its activities are to fulfil *their* purposes?' [3]

If this question—framed by Robert Dahl, Professor of Political Science at Yale University—invites no answer, it certainly deserves explanation. The traditional explanation for allowing the private power that is extended to business corporations has been summarily explained (not defended) by Professor J. K. Galbraith, as follows:

> The corporation can be private because its operations are subject to the regulation—to the presumptively comprehensive discipline— of the market. The market allows of private purpose because it keeps aligned with public purpose. The market is an expression of public preference and desire. The firm responds to the market. The firm is thus under public control. [4]

In this classical and perfect model of the consumer–producer relationship, the two sides are seen as equal and opposite forces involved in a self-righting and self-regulating arrangement in which each party can pursue a selfish aim to the advantage of the other, and also to some common good.

It seems like an ideal arrangement. The fact that the two parties are totally interdependent and bound by basically the same rules (each party responsible to itself, with injured parties having only themselves to blame) gives at least the illusion of equality and fair play. More than this, the idea of a relationship in which each party can pursue its own ends and still work to the advantage of the other has the attraction of a something-for-nothing scheme, or of a plan for perpetual motion.

And of course such schemes do not work. This one does not work according to the ideal plan for numerous reasons, any more than political democracy becomes a reality simply because individual citizens have and may use one vote—the reasons in both cases being very much the same. The power, size and resources of the average business corporation compared with those of the average individual consumer (and consumers *are* individuals, aggregated really only for statistical purposes) ensure consumers are usually on the receiving end, in every sense of the term.

Accountability and consumers

Having considered the powers and rights of business in relation to those of society, consider the rights and powers of consumers. Though their rights may be relatively few, they are comparable to those of business at least to the extent that they also relate to ownership and must also be limited by the needs of society as a whole.

It is not necessary to discuss what rights or powers should be reserved to society and what rights should be allowed to its individual or corporate members. The important thing is to acknowledge that where society reserves rights to itself, it invariably places a corresponding obligation on its members; and where members reserve rights, the opposite is usually true. There are few if any rights without corresponding obligations. For example, consumers have (full or partial) rights to either spend or save; to make their own buying decisions, including bad as well as good ones; to summon resources and use them in particular ways; and to keep, use, misuse and discard the products they have.

When consumers exercise these freedoms in certain ways, society has to pay—either in cash, and/or by limiting the freedoms allowed to others. For instance, if consumers spend much more or much less than they earn; or buy foreign goods, or bad products; or misuse products and then need medical care; or if they dump their products—then society has to pay.

Again, it is not necessary to discuss either who pays, or whether or not they pay their fair share, to make the point that society pays through the contributions of its members. Payment is made:

—in cash, by consumers as a whole—because consumers are, by definition, at least liable to foot all of society's bills, whether as consumers, taxpayers, ratepayers or in some other guise;

—in material deprivations—such as by keeping down workers' earnings; by preventing consumers from buying; or by denying citizens the benefits of a clean and pleasant environment; and/or

—in other deprivations—such as in limitations on 'the quality of life', like poor living or working conditions, ill-health or loss of amenity.

It follows from all this that, what Galbraith calls 'public preference or desire'—which in its most elementary form amounts to the consumer's satisfaction with a product—is only one of several indicators of either social or individual wellbeing, and of limited significance as a measure of the corporation's responsibilities, either to its consumers or to society at large.

Consumers are of course encouraged to think otherwise, to think of themselves as consumers and nothing much beyond. The perfect worlds of advertising, inhabited by the perfect people that consumers are supposed to want to be, suggest that anything and everything can be provided—at a cost which is only (always 'only') the price that is asked. For this, what is frequently offered is material wealth which is unhesitatingly equated with complete and untouched states of personal satisfaction.

In fact, as people and citizens, we cannot escape the evidence of each other's consumption, unless we are in complete physical or mental retreat. Nor, because we are consumers, can we avoid involvement in, or dependence on, productive work: it is only through such work we become 'eligible' to be consumers.

Equally, in return for their work (and, for a minority, in return for the work of others) most people are rewarded with tender for goods and services—for, apart from greater time or space, these are virtually the only things that money can buy. (The reward, incidentally, is not unconditional: if these goods or services give less value, less satisfaction than they might—the effect is much the same as earning less.)

It is, in other words, effectively impossible to consume only unto yourself. You cannot consume without imposing on others a wide variety of costs associated with both the production and use of goods—and they cannot consume without imposing such costs on you.

Consumer satisfaction

Consumer satisfaction has other limitations: not only is it not the only thing, it may not even be what it seems to be.

For one thing, consumers may be persuaded to buy products (which in the absence of complaint is a clear signal of satisfaction, as the producer sees it) which may do them harm. The stock list includes such things as weapons, tobacco, alcohol, motorbikes and drugs—but there are many other products besides.

It is certainly not safe to assume that the absence of control over the sale or use of products (which is characteristic for products like guns, drugs or cars) gives evidence of a product's worth. For a start, the evidence that might lead to control, if it were available, may simply not exist. For example, it is reasonable to speculate that, if the total damage caused by the use of say aspirin or asbestos products were known, then far more stringent controls might be applied to their use. Secondly, there are always political reasons for controlling some products and not others—and many of them cannot be justified objectively in terms of known benefits or costs.

Then, the satisfaction that is implicit in the (perceived or presented) appearance or image of the product, may have little to do either with the reality of the product, or with the satisfaction it is honestly able to provide. There are countless examples of this, but take vodka as a case in point:

> In the US, there are some 200 brands of vodka—despite the fact that vodka is just plain alcohol treated so that it has no distinctive character, aroma or taste—and yet the best-selling US brand is also the most expensive. Howard Cohen, the chairman of an advertising agency, has commented: 'Ninety-nine out of a hundred people could never tell the difference in vodka . . . The difference is what you perceive and we in advertising are in the business of selling images that help people to add to their overall perception of themselves.'[5]

Is there a tacit conspiracy between advertisers and consumers, by which consumers willingly pay some surcharge for the privilege of allowing themselves to be seduced into wishful thinking about themselves? At least, the evidence provided by the rise of the consumer movement suggests there is not.

Quite apart from this, the essence of much of the satisfaction that is offered lies in having an 'imposed' dissatisfaction relieved. ('Still using . . . ?'; 'Isn't it time . . . ?'; 'You owe it to . . . '; 'Would you deprive . . . ?') The marketing strategy used to play on and augment such dissatisfaction might be illustrated by analogy with a (so-far imaginary) two-stage cosmetic preparation—sold with the promise of making the user feel good, and with the instruction first to apply 'Lotion A' and later 'Lotion B'. Lotion A would be subtly formulated to make the user feel slightly itchy and uncomfortable, while Lotion B would relieve the discomfort, and perhaps replace it with a pleasant glow.

There are cases also in which the satisfaction that is promised is credible mainly because of the user's helplessness and need to believe in deliverance. They succeed because such users will also tend to interpret any failure to deliver, not as the failing of the product, but of him or herself. The point is made in this (1974) advertisement for a cosmetic cream, addressed to teenage girls: 'Have you the cheek to let him touch you? Let him feel your skin? Don't worry, the answer could be simple . . . Neutrogena.'[6]

Finally, consumer satisfaction may depend on mistaken beliefs about the performance and nature of the product, or to lack of experience with it. Does a lightbulb, a car tyre, an iron or a watch give perceptibly less satisfaction if, say, its life is degraded by 5 or 10 per cent?

The only way of knowing would be to compare the satisfaction that consumers actually obtain, with the satisfaction they would get if they had available all relevant information about the quality and value of the product in question. Clearly, there is not only a lack of such information, but those who make and market products also play upon it.

Consumer choice

If it can be reasonably assumed that consumers would make different buying decisions, if they had all relevant information available to them, can it also be assumed they would want this? Some say that consumers would prefer the more 'satisfying' illusion, and to live a quieter, less complicated life.

The answer, probably, is that while any consumer should be entitled to any information material to his or her satisfaction, the majority would not actually want much information at all. They want good value, of course, and demonstrate the value they place on trust (when they believe they are given good value) by buying the same products again and again.

But in the absence of this, consumers would probably not be prepared to obtain and use the vast quantity of information they would need; nor willingly put up with the endless slog and the mistrust that being an effective consumer might entail. What they might prefer—and what they should be entitled to expect—is a situation in which choice between products involved selection between different qualities and quantities—but was not necessary as a defence against being had. This would be possible only if reasonable standards of business behaviour were defined and then universally maintained.

2 Standards

What standards of behaviour can reasonably be expected from business; and how can such standards be defined, and compliance with them guaranteed?

There are numerous statements of the responsibilities of producers to consumers. Most of them can be discussed within the ambit of the four principles proposed in 1962 by President Kennedy, in his first consumer message to the US Congress. Kennedy proposed that consumers, as 'buyers', should have four basic rights:

(1) *The Right to Safety:* 'To be protected against marketing of goods which are hazardous to health or life.'

(2) *The Right to be Informed:* 'To be protected against fraudulent, deceitful, grossly misleading information, advertising, labelling, or other practices, and to be given the facts to make an informed choice.'

(3) *The Right to Choose:* 'To be assured, wherever possible, access to a variety of products and services at competitive prices and, in those industries in which competition is not workable and government regulation is substituted, to be assured satisfactory quality and service at fair prices.'

(4) *The Right to be Heard:* 'To be assured that consumer interests will receive full and sympathetic consideration in the formulation of government policy, and fair and expeditious treatment in its administrative tribunals.'

The main reason for restating these principles is neither to agree nor disagree with them, but to show what kind of difficulties arise when you try to turn principles into practice. Take 'the right to safety'—something which, at first sight, almost anyone would uphold. But how much protection should be given, and how could it be given without interfering unduly with those who make products or might want to use them? And how hazardous should a product be allowed to be, and does it depend on the kind of product it is? For example, should a washing machine be allowed to be as hazardous as a car? And is absolute protection to be given, or should the risk allowed be related to the likely benefit?

11

These are exactly the kinds of questions—and problems—that arise in the making and administration of law and other standards, and they partly explain why it is impossible to define specifically and comprehensively exactly what business should and should not do.

In any case, by simply cataloguing numerous prohibitions and obligations, one does nothing to ensure compliance with them. The more regulation there is, and the more complicated things become, the less people are likely to know and understand the law—and, even if they do, the more likely they probably are to ignore it. Compliance can then only be achieved through rigorous enforcement (that is, effective detection *and* prosecution)—a task which on present form many government regulatory agencies find beyond them—having neither the resources, nor often the inclination, to do more than entreat or cajole.[1]

Limitations of law and self-regulation

Having said this, it is clear that certain basic business responsibilities can and should be defined in law. It can also be taken for granted that measurement of the level of compliance with the law is basic in any social audit.

This is not to say that all law is 'good' law, either in intent or effect. To take one example, the labelling regulations which apply to the description of meat in tins, appear so non-sensically complex that they would probably be of no use at all to the average consumer, the person they should really protect. The UK Canned Meat Products Regulations 1967[2] do not require that the percentage of meat content should be declared—only that the percentage should correspond to one of the nine different descriptions that a tinned meat should be given (see Table 1).

Weaknesses in the design of legislation only compound the greater problem of its limited scope. The fact that observance of the law alone is no guarantee of responsible behaviour is underlined by the records of the Office of Fair Trading, which acts as a clearing-house for consumer complaints referred by local authorities, Citizens Advice Bureaux and other sources. In the OFT's report for 1976, some 470 000 complaints are referred to—but of these only about 14 per cent are estimated to be covered by existing criminal legislation.[3]

If there are limits to what can be achieved by law, this does not mean that self-regulation can be relied on instead—not at least in advance of fundamental reforms in company law which would make the need to assume some wider responsibilities irresistible, rather than optional.

There is certainly no reason in theory why business and other responsibilities should not be defined in standards which go beyond the law. But, in practice, self-regulation—in which business controls its own behaviour, usually following voluntary codes of practice—very rarely works well.

There have been numerous attempts to define business responsibilities using voluntary codes. Some have been better than others, but the great majority have usually failed for one or more of the following reasons.

Table 1

Trade description required	Meaning must not contain less than
Meat (for example 'Stewed Steak')	95% meat
Chopped Meat or *Cured* Meat	90% meat
Savoury Minced Meat	85% meat
Luncheon Meat	80% meat
Meat *in Gravy*	75% meat
Meat *Loaf*	65% meat
Sliced Meat with Gravy	60% meat
Meat *with Onions*	40% meat
Meat *with Vegetables in Gravy* (i.e. stewed steak with vegetables in gravy)	35% meat

By failing to provide a clear frame of reference by which conformity with given standards can be judged

Many codes or guidelines define standards of behaviour in highly generalised terms, open to the widest interpretations—and almost all are designed to be interpreted by their sponsoring bodies, rather than by those whose interests they ostensibly protect. In addition, enforcement decisions are usually taken (and sometimes kept) in secret. The result of all this is that enforcement is frequently at best expedient and at worst, downright opportunistic or corrupt.

The history of voluntary control in the advertising industry provides a fair example of this.[4] Though the industry has been publicly committed to the ideal of 'truth in advertising' for 50 years or more—at any one time 'truth in advertising' has only represented a fraction of the whole truth, albeit a fraction which in time and under pressure has somewhat increased as a proportion of the whole.

By failing to define or enforce high enough standards

Most of these codes are concerned not so much to secure 'responsible' behaviour, as to contain to a manageable level behaviour which will arouse effective complaint. As such, many codes evolve and exist mainly as means of allowing business to proceed with minimum interference from outside.

By failing to gain general acceptance

Voluntary codes can operate only where they are generally accepted. Some fail to gain full acceptance within an industry or trade; while others will *nominally* be generally observed. But, either way, the standards laid down in voluntary codes will tend—as one senior businessman has put it—'to be less than a responsible company will do under its own volition and more than an irresponsible company will do without coercion'.[5]

Of course, many of these criticisms of voluntary codes might apply also to certain laws—though more in kind than degree. And both voluntary codes and laws have other shortcomings, quite apart from any inadequacies in their design, interpretation, enforcement or scope.

One is that, by using standards to define areas of unacceptable behaviour, you also provide a framework outside of which 'anything goes', whether or not it is desirable that it should. For example, the widely (and rightly) condemned practice of pyramid selling was, in its day, vigorously defended and even promoted on the grounds that it was entirely legal. And because it was, the UK government of the day for some time shrank from publicly denouncing the practice for what it was.

There is a second related point, particularly relevant to social auditing. Neither codes nor laws were designed actually to *measure* performance; they aim only to identify behaviour which falls short of a required level. Neither codes nor laws can be used like, say, most physical standards—which you can use as sensitive measures of performance, by measuring increments of improvement above a minimum level.

Thirdly, the more regulation there is—and the more society is divided between those required to obey regulations, and those whose job it is to see they do—the more wasteful, inefficient and divided that society becomes. If people in power cannot willingly accept certain constraints, then either you settle for conflict and waste, or you remove the constraints. Or perhaps you work on the assumption that the wrong people are in power, or have more of it than is good for society, if not for them.

Finally, the wider the responsibilities of business, the less adequate 'prescribed' regulation becomes. In particular, it becomes practicably impossible to define by regulation how a company's responsibilities to one interest should relate to those of any other. For example, how could you possibly lay down a general rule to say whether, under certain circumstances, it would be more 'responsible' for a company to, say, introduce improved pollution control equipment and pass on the cost in the form of higher prices to consumers; or on the other hand to allow more pollution and so keep prices down? Such conflicts frequently arise—they were central in the *Social Audit* report on Coalite and Chemical Products Ltd—and can be resolved only as part of a political process, and not by formal regulation.

Need for information

In such cases, one can at least be sure that it should not be left to company managements, acting unilaterally, to decide what is responsible behaviour and what is not. Where there is a balance to be struck between competing interests (including always the interests of the corporation and its senior management) it should be a fundamental principle of responsible behaviour that companies propose, explain and, above all, justify their decisions.

This is not a novel proposition. It was, for instance, central to the proposals made for 'Company Law Reform', published by the last Conservative administration in July 1973.[6] Among other things, the Government White Paper stressed that 'openness in company affairs is the first principle in securing responsible behaviour' and that 'the bias must always be towards disclosure, with the burden of proof thrown on those who defend secrecy'.

But information alone is not enough. It is one thing for a company to have to provide information, to offer some justification for its activities. It is another for those activities to be in any real sense justified.

Effective accountability depends not only on the provision of information, but on a system which both sets appropriate standards and which then ensures that a company has much to gain by observing them and much to lose by not. And clearly this depends on there being effective public pressure—pressure which includes the law as a formal, if perhaps imperfect, expression of the public interest; and also effective and open channels for public approval or criticism, as an informal, and perhaps oblique, expression of it. The fact that public criticism may be oblique (and also unwelcome) in its effect, does not mean it is not constructive. Pain is an oblique way of telling the human body that something is wrong with it. Public criticism may tell the corporate body the same thing in the same way.

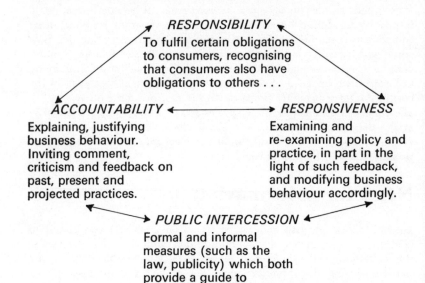

Figure 1

So, openness is important not only because it allows certain standards to be (and be seen to be) observed—or not, as the case may be. It may also greatly influence what those standards are. This is true in particular when there is no definitive and comprehensive guidance about the standards of behaviour required from business. When no such standards exist, openness might be considered both the first and last principle in securing responsible behaviour—*for if responsible behaviour cannot always be defined conclusively for what it should be, irresponsible behaviour can almost always be recognised for what it is.*

But what about the standards that do exist, and which might be relevant and credible to those involved and concerned with business behaviour? Some of the main standards that might apply to specific aspects of a company's behaviour—such as product safety or marketing—are discussed later in the book, while in the following section, there are described some of the main *kinds* of standard, with comments about their likely relevance and use.

Table 2

Examples of standards

(1) *UK statutes and regulations relating to conditions and terms of sale; product quality, quantity, safety, performance and service; price regulation and marking; competition; and provision of credit*

Sale of Goods Act 1893, as amended by the Supply of Goods (Implied Terms) Act 1973
With certain exceptions, neither manufacturers nor retailers are legally required to sell goods of any particular quality or standard. However, these acts make it an implied condition in any (oral or written) contract of sale that the goods supplied be 'reasonably fit' for the purpose for which they were supplied, and be of 'merchantable' quality, and correspond with the description by which they were sold. If and when goods do not, consumers generally have rights of redress in civil law.

The Misrepresentation Act 1967
This extends the remedies available to consumers under the above acts, in particular in cases where the seller induces the consumer to enter into a contract by negligent or fraudulent misrepresentation of material facts about the goods offered for sale.

The Trade Descriptions Act 1968
It is a criminal offence for a trader to apply a false description to any goods, or to supply any goods which are falsely described; or to give certain kinds of false indications about the price of goods; or to make certain kinds of false statements about the provision of services, facilities or accommodation.

The Weights and Measures Act 1963
It is a criminal offence to misrepresent the quantities of goods sold; or to fail to indicate the quantity of a prepackaged product. The Act may also require, by order, that certain goods are sold in prescribed quantities (for example in multiples of, say 4 oz or 100 g—rather than in the arbitrary quantities which are otherwise widely used, and which make price comparison a major feat of computation).

Fair Trading Act 1973
The Director General of Fair Trading is empowered both to collect and disseminate information about trade practices which may

'adversely affect the economic interests' of consumers and to keep under review other matters which may affect consumers' interests economically or otherwise; to initiate proposals for the introduction of secondary legislation to control practices which adversely affect consumers' economic interests; to take action against individual manufacturers or traders who persist in harmful or unfair behaviour; and to encourage the design and application of voluntary codes in business to safeguard and promote consumers' interests.

Consumer Credit Act 1974
This is aimed at comprehensive enforcement of criminal 'truth-in-lending' law, by controlling the advertising of credit and the disclosure of true interest rates—as well as the activities of creditors, brokers, debt collectors and counsellors, owners of hired goods and credit reference agencies.

Unsolicited Goods and Services Act 1971
Among other things, it is a criminal offence for traders to demand payment for unordered goods.

Trade Descriptions Act 1972
Certain imported goods must indicate the country of their origin.

Food and Drugs Act 1955
It is a criminal offence to falsely describe the nature, substance, or quality of food. The Act also regulates the ways in which food can be stored or sold.

Medicines Act 1968
It is a criminal offence to misleadingly label or advertise medicines; it requires advertisements for medicines to comply with the terms of a licence issued by the Medicines Commission in respect of each product advertised.

Consumer Protection Acts 1961 and 1971
These acts confer powers on the government to regulate the sale of dangerous goods. For example, two sets of regulations were made in 1975: The Glazed Ceramic Ware (Safety) Regulations, and The Electrical Equipment (Safety) Regulations. These acts not only provide sanctions where offences are found; they expressly and unusually provide for civil redress (see note 1 on page 24).

Independent Broadcasting Act 1973
Among other things, this act requires the Independent Broadcasting Authority to draw up and enforce standards for broadcast advertising.

Prices Act 1974
The government is allowed to regulate the price of food and other household necessities; to provide food subsidies and to make orders for price marking, including unit-pricing.

The Monopolies and Mergers Act 1965 and Monopolies and Restrictive Practices (Inquiry and Control) Act 1948
These basically allow investigations to be made into the supply, processing or exporting of goods when about one-quarter or more of the market is controlled by one firm or group; and/or into the terms, and likely effects, of any arrangement or agreement between two or more firms; where this may lead to uncompetitive conditions which may operate against the public interest (see note 2 on page 25).

The Restrictive Trade Practices Acts 1965 and 1968
All parties to any arrangement or agreement are basically required (as above) to register and justify any restrictions these may entail (see note 2 on page 25).

The Resale Prices Act 1964
It is a criminal offence for manufacturers or other suppliers to impose the minimum prices at which (most) goods are to be resold.

Other
There are many other relevant statutes apart from those listed here; for example The Insurance Companies Act 1958; The Rag, Flock and Other Filling Materials Act 1951 or The Seeds Act 1920. Over 60 statutes, for example, regulate, in one way or another the content of advertising.

Note that both impending or proposed legislation may provide useful standards for reference purposes. For instance, some years may elapse between the enactment and introduction/enforcement of the provisions of many acts (for example the Consumer Credit and Equal Pay Acts); and measures may be proposed in 'Green Papers' (raising issues) and in White Papers (trying to resolve them)—and all of these may provide useful guidelines for assessing a company's performance. Even repealed legislation may provide guidelines: for example, The Code of Industrial Relations Practice associated with the now-repealed Industrial Relations Act 1971 outlines standards which, if inadequate today, are still useful for reference purposes.

(2) *Actual or impending legislation overseas*

Having or likely to have a direct bearing on UK policy or practice

For example, a decision or a regulation or a directive from the EEC—whether proposed or finalised, and whether optional or binding on member states of the community—would directly affect the UK.

Having or likely to have an indirect bearing on UK policy or practice

For example, requirements under the US National Highway and Traffic Safety Act 1966 would not only have influenced the shape of legislation in the UK and elsewhere (and therefore the shape of products covered by such legislation). It has also made direct requirements for UK cars exported to the US—which may well bear comparison with standards which apply to the UK domestic market. The existence of this particular law has certainly created a double standard : UK motor manufacturers have for some time supplied one standard for the home market and another higher one for the US and elsewhere. Specifically, there are no UK requirements for bumper strength or design—while there are in the US—and in such cases reference may be made to both the higher and lower standard, when assessing a company's performance.

Having no obvious bearing on UK policy, but nevertheless illustrating alternative approaches to common or possible problems

For example, the US Refrigerator Safety Act 1956 effectively prohibits the sale of any refrigerator 'unless it is equipped with a device enabling the door thereof to be opened from the inside'. Here, the problem of accidents with children, who suffocate inside locked (usually dumped) fridges, was recognised in US law which anticipated any such requirement in the UK. The relatively early recognition of this problem in the US (perhaps due to the fact there were more and bigger fridges there than elsewhere) gave early warning of a standard which would later be seen to be needed in other countries as well.

(3) *Codes of Practice*

Semi-statutory codes

There are a number of codes which, though they have no binding legal force, would (if breached) provide powerful *prima facie* evidence of misconduct in law. Sometimes these codes of practice fill in the gaps in the law. For example, the amazing Fish and Meat Spreadable Products Regulations 1968 (made under The Food and Drugs Act

1955) specify that 'salmon spread' must contain at least 70 per cent of salmon and that 'salmon paste' contain at least 70 per cent of fish—but requires only that salmon must 'characterise' the paste. However, there is a code of practice agreed with the Food Manufacturers Federation which says that, in salmon paste, there should be at least 25 per cent of salmon, the remaining 45 per cent consisting of any fish.[7]

Another example of a semi-statutory code of practice is the broadcast advertising code administered by the Independent Broadcasting Authority. The code itself has no force in law—though the IBA does have a statutory duty to draw up and enforce a code of advertising standards.

Sub-statutory codes

For want of a better description, this term has been used to describe a number of codes which, in effect, operate in place of statutory controls. In theory, these codes are entirely voluntary; in practice they are observed, partly as a means of keeping statutory controls at bay.

For instance, several codes of practice have been produced by industry or business 'in consultation with' (that is, under some pressure from) the government's Office of Fair Trading. (An explanation for this is the unwillingness of government to take responsibility for control—for financial or political reasons, or both—in circumstances in which it nevertheless wants to see less criticism and complaint about business—and, by implication, of itself.)

The Office of Fair Trading has a statutory duty to encourage the development of such codes, and has been involved in (or has influenced) the design and/or administration of codes on advertising practice; the supply and servicing of electrical goods; the repair, servicing and sale of cars; footwear quality and repairs; furniture; dry cleaning and laundering. The enforcement of these codes is left to the organising industry. However, checks have been made by the OFT, whose sanction on their observance is the (more or less real, but always unwelcome) threat of legislation.

Codes backed by professional sanctions

These include, notably, the codes and rules laid down by professional and semi-professional bodies (such as the Royal Institution of British Architects) which are enforced under threat of loss of privilege, public criticism or expulsion from membership.

Strictly voluntary codes

There are other codes, agreed within a company or industry, which are intended mainly as guidance; their effectiveness depends not only on the standards required but on the co-operation of those who are expected to meet them. For instance, in the 'Statement of Trading Standards', issued by Curry's Ltd, is the requirement: 'It is the responsibility of Curry's sales staff to make sure that a customer thoroughly understands the features and performance of a product before making a purchase'. Regardless of the intention of such a requirement, it is clear that the interpretations put on it might vary considerably.

(4) *Product standards and specifications*

General design, performance or other specifications

There are many bodies which produce such specifications, most with a view to product standardisation and/or certification as well as quality compliance. The principal standard-making body in the UK is the British Standards Institution (BSI). Other major authorities include the American Society for Testing and Materials (ASTM); the Deutscher Normenausschuss (DIN), the Association Française de Normalisation (NF); and the USSR State Committee for Standards, Measurements and Measuring Instruments (GOST). The International Organisation for Standardisation (ISO) prepares internationally agreed standards.

Several thousand products, components, processes and procedures are covered by British Standards. In addition, over 200 products carry the BSI 'Kitemark' certificate, indicating that production samples (as well as the original design) have been sample-tested for compliance. British Standards vary in their requirements—for example, they are notably tough for certain life-saving equipment, and apparently far less so for many other products. They are all intended to ensure that goods are reasonably fit for the purpose for which they were intended.

There are many other standardisation and approvals bodies. They include the Design Council, British Electro-Technical Approvals Board, Retail Trading Standards Association, the British Gas Corporation, and also a number of trade, professional and research organisations.

Purchasing specifications

Many large corporate consumers have either modified existing standards, or developed their own, to be able to specify to suppliers exactly what qualities and quantities they require. These corporate consumers include private and public corporations; central government; the armed forces; local government; and some trade, professional and other organisations.

Remarkably little information is available in the UK about the work of central or local government as a corporate consumer—though the

Ministry of Defence has published a number of standards relating to both manufacturing processes and products, for military procurement purposes.

By contrast, extensive information is available on standardisation in the US, notably from the Department of Commerce, General Services Administration, and the Department of Defence.

(5) *Performance criteria*

Performance measured as improvement over time, or in relation to the performance of other, comparable companies

If you can measure performance then, with adequate data, you can also measure performance over time—to see whether there have been changes, either for better or worse. For example, does the level and nature of complaints made in 1978 show an improvement or deterioration over 1977? Has the price of a product kept pace with, exceeded or been lower than, say, the energy, labour, material and other costs involved in making it?

In the same way, performance of the one company can be compared with performance of others. In the two examples above, for instance, the performance of the subject company could be compared with that of its principal competitors.

Performance in objective tests

The performance of a product can be assessed against either a known standard, or against the performance of other products, or both. Such tests may be carried out not only by consumer organisations, such as Consumers' Association, but also by any one of the bodies identified as purchasing organisations in 4 above.

Performance in relation to attainable standards

The tests referred to immediately above may not include an assessment against standards known to be attainable but not actually attained. For instance, the publication *Motoring Which?* (from Consumers' Association) has reported on tests of hundreds of cars—though all comparisons have been between petrol/diesel-driven vehicles, simply because electrically driven cars (though feasible, like several other alternative designs) have not been available to test.

Performance in relation to the organisation's own stated objectives

Finally, performance may be judged against the claims an organisation makes for itself, and the promises it makes to others.

Note that promises frequently conflict: a company may advertise 'more profit for you' to dealers, and unjustifiably advertise 'more value for you' to consumers. Similarly, profit is something to be advertised and emphasised to shareholders and creditors, rather than in statements to employees.

Statements of intent may be formal and binding, as in a company's legal objects. Or they may be less so—for example, in corporate advertising. Thus, it is the principal legal object of the Advertising Standards Authority Ltd to promote and enforce 'the highest standards of advertising in all media'; while the ITT Corporation implies another kind of standard when it advertises : 'The International Corporation was not organised with a single profit-making purpose to itself, nor with the desire of imposing American practices in its foreign activities . . .'[8]

(6) *Other standards*

Minority requirements
There are numerous cases in which more and less formal standards give expression to minority needs. For example, the 'gluten-free' symbol which appears on some foods is the 'standard' form of protection available to people who suffer from coeliac disease. By contrast, the 'standard', flesh-pink colour of sticking plasters might be considered 'standard' only for wounded Caucasians.

Minority interests
There is also a variety of more and less widely accepted 'ethical' standards. Thus, there are no fundamental legal constraints (not at least in UK law) which affect such things as arms manufacture, asset stripping, animal tests, employment conditions in UK companies overseas, or the marketing of baby food and other products in the third world. Yet all such issues are of great concern, at least to minority interests—and, in any social audit report, should be recognised as such.

Notes
(1) Of the various statutes and regulations described here, only the Sale of Goods Act, the Misrepresentation Act and the Consumer Protection Acts expressly provide for civil liability. Claims for damages cannot proceed automatically following conviction under the other, criminal, statutes listed : they may or may not be admissible, depending on the circumstances of the case and, probably, the disposition of the judge.

However, under the Criminal Evidence Act 1968, proof of a criminal conviction will be accepted as *prima facie* proof of the facts on which that conviction was based, in any subsequent civil action.

In addition, under the provisions of s.1 of the Criminal Justice Act 1972, an order for compensation may be made, for personal injury, loss or damage, following a conviction for a criminal offence (for example, under the Trade Descriptions Act 1968).[9]

(2) For more detailed information, please refer to the checklist at the end of Chapter 7 (pages 90 to 99).

Test of public acceptance

Clearly, it is much easier to report on business behaviour when there are formal and generally accepted standards and when you can assess a company's performance by reference to them. But this does not mean that business performance cannot or should not be assessed when no such standards exist.

What matters is that a company's behaviour is fairly and accurately described *for what it is*. The absence of standards against which to assess this performance—that is the absence of any formal expression of public and other expectations of business—certainly cannot be taken to mean that anything goes. For there are at least implied standards for all business performance. What is implied is that business behaviour can stand the test of general public approval—and what is suggested here is that it should.

Where no formal standards or laws exist, it is quite probably all the more important that business performance be tested against the public's reaction to it. If the public generally can accept the reality of business behaviour for what it is, then well and good—and if not, there is a case for improvement or change.

But business accountability can never become a reality unless and until this test is applied—and it is the most basic objective in a social audit to apply it.

3 Information

The first part of this chapter explains what information you may need; the second suggests how to obtain and use it.

Information necessary

A social audit is concerned ultimately with four questions: the first two concern the causes of a company's behaviour, while the other two relate to effects. Each of these four main questions (below left) suggests further questions (below right). And these, in turn, lead to more and more specific questions about what companies do and why.

(1) What does the company aim to do?

    (i) What are the company's intentions?
    (ii) What influences are there on the company?

(2) How does the company set about this?

    (i) How is the company organised?
    (ii) What procedures are defined and used and resources applied?

(3) What does the company actually do?

    (i) To what extent does the company achieve its intended goals?
    (ii) How do these goals affect the interests of different stakeholders?
    (iii) What unintended or incidental effects occur?

(4) What might or should the company do?

    (i) Modify its goals?
    (ii) Modify the means used to attain these goals?
    (iii) Account for its behaviour?

The weight of these issues varies. For example, what a company does is ultimately more important than either how or why it does it—and a social auditor's report should reflect this. However, at the research stage, all factors should be taken into account.

The following table suggests further questions relating to each of the main issues identified above. These general questions may be used in conjuction with the Checklists at the end of chapters 4 to 8, in which specific questions have been raised about the design, manufacture, packaging, marketing and use of different products.

Table 3

---

(1) What does the company aim to do?

(i) Intentions of the company

—Does the company have either any overall objective or any specific policies which would or might affect its performance?

—How are these objectives expressed? Are they formally defined, and are they specific and comprehensive?

—How would they be likely to be interpreted and enforced? In their normal operation is adequate provision made for checking compliance?

—What evidence is there of commitment to company or management policies by employees and by their representative bodies? Is there full understanding and acceptance of policies both by those concerned about, and those likely to be affected by, their working or failure to work?

—How did the policy evolve, and what changes have been made to it? Do any changes made give evidence of the firm's ability to identify and correct failures, and to take thorough and effective action to prevent them recurring?

—What evidence of intent can be found in the attention given by the firm to the conduct of the operations of others on which it may directly or indirectly depend?

Comments

A company's objectives may be expressed in its memorandum and articles of association; in policy statements, prospectuses, resolutions; in published statements such as advertising and product literature; in speeches, interviews, announcements and articles; in petitions or applications made by the company (for example, in support of, or against, planning and other proposals); in internal communications and documents, including minutes of evidence, contracts, specifications, and proposals, agreements or instructions. Evidence of intent may be seen also in appointments, investment decisions, acquisition and divestment and in trade affiliations and other activities.

Evidence from such sources should be collected and analysed with a view to establishing (a) whose interests, or what interests, are affected—and to what extent they are promoted, retarded or overlooked—by what the company does; and (b) whether the company's policies work in fact as they are intended or said to work.

An increasing number of larger companies publish formal statements of their overall objectives and/or of their commitments to consumer and other interests. The existence of such a statement, in itself, may mean nothing: some are window-dressing, others not.

Among others, the British Institute of Management (1976) has surveyed major companies' statements or codes.[1] Two examples quoted in this report are: (1) The Articles of Association of Scott-Bader Co. Ltd (an employee co-ownership) require the Company to 'produce goods not only beneficial to customers of the Company at a fair price and as high a quality as possible but also for the peaceful purposes and general good of mankind'. The Company has reportedly turned down government (military?) contracts in pursuing this principle. (2) The principles and objectives of the Quaker Oats Company require that they 'create and provide an increasingly diversified line of consumer products and services that (i) satisfy genuine needs and desires (ii) have characteristics of distinctiveness that permit marketing under brand or proprietary names; and that (iii) appeal to large and fast-growing segments and have the potential to become market leaders'.

The implication, if not the exact significance, of these two statements is clear enough—as is the contrast between them. However, there are no formal, generally accepted standards by which to judge such statements. If they are precise enough to mean anything, then they set standards in themselves.

Ultimately, such statements stand as a rough measure of a company's intent to serve itself; or to serve itself by serving others; or to serve others even to the extent of denying its own commercial interests.

(ii) Influences on the company
—What standards affecting the company's policy or practice are applied?

—What kinds of pressure are there on the company either to observe or ignore any particular standard?

—What degree of pressure may be applied by such means, and how easily or effectively may it be resisted?

Comment

These three questions sum up the company's response to a considerable range and number of factors which can influence the way it acts. The company's basic intent may be advanced or retarded by such things as its own standing—for example its own strength, size, profitability, structure and organisation, in relation to its competition. It may be affected by the company's origins and affiliations—such as by religious or political connections, family involvements, cross-linkings of directorships; and by the nature of ownership and control in the company.

The company's behaviour will certainly be influenced by the requirements of law, and probably also by standards and codes of practice (details in Chapter 2, pages 17 to 25). Similarly, a company's conduct will be influenced by the terms of its agreements with employees and their representative bodies, with suppliers and corporate consumers; and with competitors, either directly or through industry-wide agreements.

Finally, there may be informal, external constraints—and notably the possibility of exposure to criticism from competitors, the press, public or special interests.

Where a company would not incline to observe certain standards—through lack of self-interest or self-discipline—two factors will particularly influence the standards it actually observes. The first is the standard being seen to be observed by the company's competitors—by consumers, or by employees or other interests, as well as by officials from regulatory agencies. The second factor is what these interests or observers know—and are allowed to know—about the standards the company actually does and might observe. A company may, in other words, either achieve compliance with a standard, or disguise evidence of non-compliance. Both methods are used.

(2) How does the company set about this?

(i) Organisation

—Is the structure and capability of the company (in all elements of the organisation, including design, manufacture, quality control, marketing, etc.) sufficient to ensure the implementation of policy?

—Are policies clearly understood as authoritative statements of intent at all levels—and do they establish principles that provide a basis for action at all levels?

—Do policies fully explain the company's commitment, and give reasons for that commitment that are appreciated by all concerned?

—Are responsibility and authority for implementing policies

appropriately assigned in the company? Are responsibilities for implementing all specific provisions clearly assigned to specific people or functions, and are all those involved given sufficient authority?

—By what authority may changes in policy be made, and what arrangements exist for changes in policy to be proposed and evaluated?

—Is there adequate communication between all those responsible for the implementation of policies, and are all changes in policy effectively communicated to all concerned?

—To what extent are policies communicated to, and implemented by, agents and others outside, on whom the company depends—and by what means is their compliance with company standards assured?

—Are such agents notified in all cases of non-compliance and what remedial action is taken?

—Are such agents explicitly required to notify the company immediately when deviations from standards are known to have occurred, or when defects or hazards are known to be associated with the provision of materials or services to the company?

Comments

These questions are far from comprehensive—not surprising considering the variety of products and policies there are. They serve mainly to make the basic point that there is no point in having a policy which cannot be implemented—or in making commitments which cannot be honoured—and that no policy can be implemented unless: (i) a company is appropriately organised to do so; (ii) responsibilities and authority are actually assigned, rather than simply discussed and aired; and (iii) everyone concerned can understand and accept the responsibilities they are expected to assume.

The consequences of having a policy but failing to ensure that it works may well be worse than having no policy at all. This is because the existence of a policy may inspire confidence which is unjustified—and which may lead to the neglect of precautions and the taking of risks. (A clear example of this, relating to the safety of employees—who had wrongly been led to believe their company used no carcinogenic materials in the manufacture of tyres—is discussed in *Social Audit on Avon*, pages 34 and 38.)

The words 'appropriate' and 'sufficient' recur unexplained in the questions listed above—obviously because no one kind of organisation can be considered right in all cases. However, evidence of sufficiency (or lack of it) may be found (i) in documents used to explain, define or review the organisation adoped; (ii) by reference to the procedures and resources used by the company in support of the organisation adopted; (iii) in company evaluations of the effectiveness of the working of policies, in practice; and in (iv) the findings of internal enquiries relating to the control or audit of the organisation and procedures used in support of a particular policy.

The emphasis on such audit procedures is made in the belief that no policy can be intended or expected to work satisfactorily unless checked and controlled—and therefore that the effectiveness of such measures indicates perhaps better than anything else what determination there is to make a policy work well.

(ii) Procedures and Resources
—What procedures are followed when policies are drawn up, modified and reviewed? In particular, is there adequate and effective consulatation with, and/or representation of, all parties affected and concerned?

—Are appropriate procedures and resources applied in the recruitment, selection, training, reward and discipline of employees—as these might affect the successful implementation of policies?

—Are appropriate procedures and resources applied in the organisation of work—including working conditions and environment, work methods, work satisfaction, job evaluation, work assignment and job opportunity, supervision and control, and facilities both for working and for workers?

—Are appropriate procedures and resources applied in the case of handling and processing of materials and the use of equipment?

—What procedures are used in, and resources applied to, the systematic control over the operation of such practices by means of integrated or separate audit functions?

Comments
There is no one measure of the value of the many different procedures used, or resources applied, in these different areas—and sufficiency can probably best be judged by reference to reviews, evaluations and audits of activities, described in items (i) to (iv) in the comments above.

There exist numerous indicators and sources of information which may provide direct or indirect evidence of failure or potential failure of adopted (or neglected) procedures in these areas. Production problems and achievements may for example be referred to in minutes of meetings between employee representatives and management, in inspection and other records and logs, or in supervisors' reports; while some indication of conditions of work may be given in statistics of labour turnover, accidents, absenteeism or industrial action—all of which should be regularly maintained.

Several examples of the relevance of such information are given in the report *Social Audit on Avon*. For instance, reference is made to the effect of inadequate training (acknowledged in the company's Survey of Training Needs) on the quality of products (pages 41–44) ; and to the use of piece-work rates for work which required particular attention and care (page 60).

All such items might be covered in the company's own audit procedures, referred to above. These control systems—or the appropriate parts of them—should be examined with a view to finding out (i) to what extent they may be relied on to accurately measure performance in implementing policy; and to identify inadequate performance and the reasons for it; (ii) to what extent they may be effectively used as a means of remedying inadequacy.

Finally, the significance of any lack of an effective system of feedback and control should be related to the actual and possible consequences of allowing different operations to be carried out unchecked.

(3) What does the company actually do?

(i) To what extent does the company achieve its intended goals?

—Which standards (goals) have been met, and which not—and what level of (non) compliance is involved?

—What is the significance of any failures in indicating the firm's priorities and the commitment and competence of its officers—or the adequacy of the organisation, procedures and resources involved?

—What are the consequences of failure, expressed in terms of penalties faced, potential or actual harm to consumer and other interests, and remedies applied?

Comment

Bear in mind that, although compliance with a goal or standard is often formally defined in 'pass-or-fail' terms, in practice more sensitive measures may be found. To give an example : in a (1975) Department of Trade report on a car-dealing and property company, John Willment Automobiles, it is alleged that the company infringed the law on 397 separate occasions, between 1964 and 1972. But, while this company was said to be 'consistently among the very worst offenders of all limited companies', the Department of Trade decided *not* to prosecute, in effect because it found no evidence that dishonesty was involved. [2]

Equally, distinctions may be made between cases in which come panies were found to have been :

(1) Convicted for non-compliance, and been punished more or less.
(2) Prosecuted, but not convicted.

(3) Received a 'prosecution warning' or notice of infraction, but not been prosecuted.

(4) Received public criticism from the appropriate enforcement authority (for non-compliance) but not been prosecuted.

(5) Operating within the letter, if not apparently within the spirit, of the law.

(6) Operating apparently within the letter and spirit of the law.

(7) Operating apparently beyond the requirements of the law or standard, or significantly in advance of proposed standards or laws.

Comparable distinctions may often be made in judging the extent to which other (non-legal) requirements have been met.

The other points listed in question 3 (i) above are largely covered by comments under headings 2 (i) and (ii) above; and 3 (ii) and (iii) below.

(ii) How do goals affect the interests of different stakeholders?

—How does the company's performance compare with its own past performance, and with the performance of similar companies engaged in comparable activities—in relation to any major standard affecting the production, distribution, consumption or disposal of its products?

—How has the company responded in dealing with complaints relating to its products—whether addressed specifically to the company, or made generally of activities in which it is involved?

Comment

As society's expectations of the company must relate to what is known about what the company does, the answers to such questions might still leave much unsaid. However, the object here is to establish what response is made where some response is actually called for—while the questions listed in (3) (iii) below relate more to responses which should be called for.

The standards referred to above are listed by type in chapter 2 (page 17), while specific examples of standards which might apply are given in the checklists following Chapters 4 to 8.

Bear in mind here that standards—that is formal and authoritative 'yardsticks'—may not exist. This should not matter, provided (i) a description is given of the performance the company actually gives; (ii) this is relevant; and (iii) the company's performance is described in relation to performance that might reasonably be given or required. (Obviously, the value and credibility of an assessment will depend on the auditor referring to reasonable standards, fully explained.)

(iii) What unintended or incidental effects occur?

—What secondary effects do or might be expected to occur as a result of (i) failure to implement policy, as intended; (ii) failure to appreciate the actual and/or full effects of pursuing policies as intended; or (iii) failing to modify policy to correct unwanted effects?

—What type of effects would be involved; what systems or communities might be affected; and what would be the magnitude and significance of the effects?

Comments

The number and range of possible secondary effects is considerable— in that a company's consumer practices might affect, or be affected by, almost any action the company might take.

There is no simple or single method by which these many different effects can be either anticipated, classified or reviewed. However, the methods used by US government agencies in the preparation of 'Environmental Impact Statements' suggest one possible approach— and one which is almost certainly well in advance of any comparable methods for examining the impact of business on the community.

At the same time, this approach can be used only to examine what the consequences of particular decisions are or may be. It provides a framework for assessing or making decisions—but without necessarily providing irresistible evidence to show whether decisions are 'right' or 'wrong'.

The method and objective of the approach ultimately involve no more than asking all the right questions. In this context, these questions might relate to:

Type of impact involved

—*Social impacts*

Physical composition (for example, of the community, in terms of the population size, density, stratification and migration; or of personal or communal property and facilities, in terms of their availability, accessibility, character, distribution, value and variety)

Social organisation (for example, rate, pattern and type of land use; mode, availability and accessibility of transport; use of amenities, recreational and other facilities)

Individual and social integrity (for example, physical health and safety; and social/psychological well-being, including sense of identity, integration, purpose and fulfilment.

—*Environmental impacts*

Terrestrial and aquatic communities (for example, common, vulnerable, valuable and/or unique plant, fish or animal species)

Energy and natural resources (availability, conservation, use and reuse thereof)

Waste disposal (for example, quality of air and upper atmosphere; water quality and quantity; and generation and disposal of solid wastes)

—Economic impacts
Production related (for example, employment, investment, productivity, competition, prices)

Sales related (for example, income, public expenditure and control, inflation, balance of payments)

Areas of consumer-related impacts
Production-related systems For example, nature and extent of research affecting product design and improvement, and development of new products and byproducts; changes in the use of materials relating to, say, availability, cost, toxicity or performance; and changes in production methods involving changes in efficiency, energy use, safety or cost.

Distribution systems For example, changes in the mode, cost or type of packaging; changes in stock movements or control; changes in the mode, frequency or cost of transportation; changes affecting wholesale or retailing activity; and in the methods, costs and character of marketing.

Consumption and use characteristics For example, safety, durability, utility, appearance, availability, variety and size, weight, shape, and price of products; changes in purchasing patterns and in number or composition of consumers for whom products are accessible; and changes in consumption patterns, including use, misuse, repair and reuse and abuse.

Disposal characteristics For example, changes in frequency or methods of product disposal; changes in the amount and type of waste produced; and opportunities for the reclamation, reuse or recycling of waste products.

Nature and extent of impact
Magnitude For example, great, moderate, small; short, medium or long-term; international, national, local; constant, frequent, occasional, etc.

Significance For example, adverse or beneficial; unique or common-place; possible or inevitable; reversible or irreversible; known or unknown; calculable or incalculable, etc.

This list is not, and could never be, complete. It may be helpful as a framework and in prompting questions in significant areas—but it is left to those carrying out a review to frame precisely the right questions in the appropriate degree of detail.

(4) What might or should the company do?

—In what way(s) might the company modify its goals; why should it do so; and how and at what cost might this be done?

—In what way(s) might the company modify the means used to achieve particular objectives; why should it do so; and how and at what cost might this be done?

—In what way(s) might the company account more appropriately for its behaviour, given the responsibilities it does or might assume?

Comment

The value of any recommendation that the company should adopt a particular policy or standard will be so much the greater if (i) the case for change is fully explained; (ii) an assessment of the costs and benefits involved is made; and (iii) the company's response to any proposed change is given and evaluated.

More than this, the audit report should identify all issues and questions needing further study or clarification. The report should state also whether any significant information is missing, or has been withheld; and an explanation should be given of the nature of such information and any reasons given for withholding it.

In most situations, it may be taken as axiomatic that the responsibility for providing necessary information—or for explaining in full why this cannot be done—lies with the company management.

Fact finding

So much for the kind of information that may be needed. But what about getting and using it?

The principal sources of specific information about a company include the management, the employee (union) representatives, government (regulatory) agencies, competitors, suppliers (including agents) and purchasers (including wholesalers and retailers). Help from employee representatives may be negotiated independently, but the chances of getting significant information from other sources depends greatly on securing management co-operation.

Since social auditors have no authority and cannot (and certainly should not) guarantee to use company information for company purposes and on the company's terms, the propects of management co-operation are not overwhelmingly good.

Several factors would influence whether a company agreed to co-operate—and to what extent—whether or not it wanted to. The competence, resources, experience, reputation and approach of the auditors would all be important. But the most important thing—and one which relates closely to the determination of the auditors to carry out a review, if not with co-operation then without—is the question of the consequences for the company of refusing to give information that might reasonably be requested.

In the traditional financial audit or assessment, the refusal to give information may well reflect damagingly on the company being examined. For instance, in a 1973 report on the Distillers Company Ltd (DCL), the stockbrokers, George Henderson, commented: 'Excessive secrecy is often a sign of weakness and, at present, we have to make too many estimates about DCL to be enthusiastic in recommending the company to an investor'.[3] And, just as a refusal to give information in a financial audit may lead to suspicion of failure or fraud—particularly if the refusal is not reasonably explained—so it must in a social audit.

The time may come—whether or not social audits become an established thing—when social accountability is more of a reality than a sham. In the meantime, any serious attempt to obtain and publish relevant information about what companies do, and why, must be welcome.

With this in mind, it may be worth outlining what general sources of information there are, and how forthcoming and useful they may be. (Details of more specific sources of information—for example relating to marketing or design—are given in the chapters which follow. Readers wanting further *general* information might refer to standard publications on this subject.[4])

The remarks made in the following section presuppose that enquiries are being made about a company by a competent auditor (that is, reasonably skilled and experienced, independent and exercising due integrity and care[5]) but acting neither on the instruction nor invitation of the company, nor in any official capacity.

Table 4

Sources of information

(1) Company

—*Published material*—for example, annual reports, press notices, house journal, etc.—should be freely available.

—*Other documents*—for example, minutes of meetings, instructions to staff, policy statements, programme reviews, etc.—expect to be asked, 'What do you want if for ?' and expect a refusal when disclosure would be likely to cause embarrassment; or when data requested include personal information about individual employees, or commercially 'sensitive' information. Without prior agreement to co-operate, companies may refuse disclosure of any price sensitive information not available to shareholders (that is, in the annual report)—in accordance with the conditions of their Stock Exchange listing.

—*Designated spokespersons*—for example, press and public relations personnel, senior managers—spokespersons are usually designated not because they are necessarily well-informed, but because of their proven or presumed ability to protect and enhance the reputation of the company. Their willingness to disclose information will depend largely on their judgement of whether a report of non-cooperation will be more or less embarrassing than the disclosure of any information requested.

—*Other employees*—for example, individual management or shop floor personnel, approached privately—their attitude to disclosure varies predictably. Co-operation will depend on such factors as their standing with the company, and yours; the degree of embarrassment disclosure might cause; and whether information can/will be traced to source.

—*Employee representatives*—for example, union or staff association representatives—co-operation can never be taken for granted, but should usually be given. Representatives will be less likely to want to discuss consumer issues than others, relating to employee welfare—but may provide significant information, for example about training and manning.

—*Agents or consultants*—for example, past or present advertising agents, design consultants, etc.—as with spokespersons or other employees above.

—*Former employees*—for example, individuals identified through personal contact, or through trade directories, etc.—generally helpful, though not always informed on up-to-date issues.

(2) Industry related

—*Trade or employer's association or professional body*—unlikely to be able or willing to provide specific information: willingness to help can depend on dominance of company within the body or association.

—*Competitors*—may provide useful background information (for example, about processes or technologies used in an industry) but generally do unto others as they would be done by.

—*Wholesalers, dealers, suppliers*—predictably, the greater their distance from, and independence of the company, the more likely they are to give information—and the less likely that information is to be of great use.

—*Industrial purchasers*—like competitors or suppliers.

—*Standard-making bodies*—not likely to have or give much information about specific companies. Minutes and related documents from meetings of standard-making committees are likely to be treated as confidential, but may be obtainable through consumer/minority representatives on the committee. British Standards Institution regularly tests samples of 'Kitemarked' products, following procedures described in a 'Scheme of Supervision and Control'. BSI treats both the test results and these schemes as confidential.

(3) Special interest organisations

—*Consumer organisations*—generally helpful, sometimes slow. May be guarded in providing information directly relating to published data. Some may find it difficult to find time or resources to help.

—*Academic sources*—usually helpful; but may be inhibited through connections with government or industry. Lack of decisiveness and dislike of controversy can cause problems.

—*Research or lobby organisations*—marked contrast between

established and establishment organisations—such as the Automobile Association or the Royal Society for the Prevention of Accidents— and others, such as Friends of the Earth. The latter tend to be more helpful and more open.

—*Local or special interest groups*—the quality of their information varies a good deal, but their response to requests for information are generally helpful and good.

(4) Government and others

—*Published data*—such as reports from regulatory agencies or from committees of enquiry; parliamentary papers, legal proceedings, etc. Finding exactly what you think you want may be both frustrating and time-consuming. Having found it, you may be lucky—it may actually be what you do want. But you may also be defeated by the wealth of gloss, generalisations, understatement and equivocation.

—*Unpublished data*—for example, routine reports by inspectors from central or local government agencies; minutes of meetings; statements of enforcement policies and procedures; analyses and interpretations of business behaviour, etc. (These are the data which contain the meat which is so often minced, coloured, flavoured and tenderised before being offered for public consumption.) In theory, such data cannot legally be obtained from central government agencies unless its release is 'authorised'. In practice authorisation is the exception to a general rule of excessive and sometimes absurd secrecy. The legal justification for this exists not only in the all-embracing provisions of Section 2 of the Official Secrets Act 1911, but also under specific requirements for secrecy in over 60 different statutes. For further information refer to *Social Audit* No. 1 (pp. 53– 64); No. 2 (pp. 3–18); Nos. 3, 4, 5, 6 (numerous isolated references) and Nos. 7 and 8 (especially p. 2).)

—*Individual government employees*—employees and ex-employees alike are bound by the provisions of the Official Secrets Act and as the former Home Secretary, Roy Jenkins, has observed: 'It would be almost impossible (for a civil servant or minister) on a strict observance of the . . . Act to hold any intelligent conversation at all which was not self-consciously on an extremely remote range of subjects'.[6] However, in practice, some civil servants will give information, just as would individual company employees.

—*Overseas data*—useful background information may be obtained, for example, through the EEC and occasionally from individual governments abroad. It is worth noting that information of the kind held secret in the UK may sometimes be freely obtained elsewhere. For example, much of the information listed above is publicly available in the US—partly because of its more liberal traditions on disclosure of information, and partly because access is often guaranteed under the provisions of US Freedom of Information legislation. Occasionally, it is possible to secure information in the US which directly relates to UK practice, when such information cannot be obtained here. *Social Audit* has, for instance, obtained US reports on hygiene conditions, quality control standards, etc. in UK factories, and even a few 'secret' UK government reports, all on the public record in the US.

(5) Commercial and other information agencies

—*Press, media and related services*—for example, national or local papers, radio and TV reports, trade and professional journals; press cuttings services etc. Generally easily obtained, though not always easy to locate. Journalists themselves will often help, particularly if professionally or otherwise interested in the enquiry in progress.

—*Other sources*—for example, registers, catalogues, buying guides, yearbooks, directories, etc. These often contain invaluable information. Get them from major reference libraries—and always ask if you cannot find what you want. Librarians are almost always very helpful, and often almost absurdly knowledgeable. Their skills are probably very underestimated and largely underemployed.

True and fair view

Finally, how should such information be processed and presented in an audit report?

The basic requirement, very briefly, is to use only relevant and reliable information to present a clear, complete, accurate and fair account. There is of course much more than this to be said. Indeed, much of it has been said—for example in *Standards for Audit of Governmental Organisations, Programs, Activities and Functions*[7] among other audit guidelines.

However, in the view of the problem of obtaining information, there would be little point in elaborating here on the question of processing and presenting it. To do so would be to count chickens before they were hatched, if not eggs before they got laid.

Part Two—Products

This part of the report discusses and outlines some of the principal indicators by which the competence and commitment of producers to act 'responsibly' might be judged. The framework followed (anti-clockwise) is illustrated in Figure 2.

Each of the next five chapters begins with narrative which explains and outlines the main issues involved. These chapters each end with a checklist, which includes a list of questions that might be raised in a social audit—and also some comments on interpretation, standards and principal sources of information.

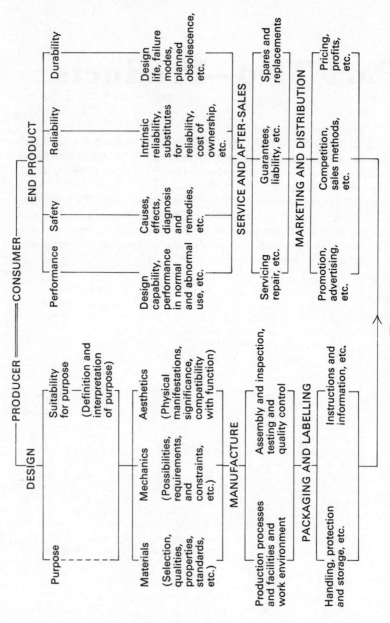

Figure 2

4 Design

Purpose of design

What is a product worth? Is a product really worth making? It seems fundamental to both the definition and the pursuit of social purpose to raise such questions—even if they are extremely difficult, perhaps impossible, to resolve.

Tradition has it that market value determines what a product is worth. This tells you what certain consumers, for a variety of reasons, think a product is worth to them, and what certain producers think it worth making a product for. It does not get to the real point at issue: does a product add value to an individual's life and to society generally and, if so, how much value and at what cost?

To assess the worth of a product in these terms one needs to know (i) what (subjective and objective) value that product has to the consumer; (ii) what other benefits and costs are associated with that product's use; and (iii) what costs and benefits are associated with the production of the product.

Value to consumer

The problem with assessing the value of a product to the consumer is that value depends not only on what the product is or does, but also on the use it is put to. For example, the benefit that an elderly, isolated person would get from a telephone would be likely to be very different to the benefit felt by an office worker using the same product for internal communication. Still, an estimate of product value might be attempted by taking into account (i) the nature, (ii) the degree, and (iii) the scope of the benefit that a product would be likely to bring.

The *nature* of a benefit might be expressed in terms of the dispensability or indispensability of a product; that is, in terms of what it provides in relation to human want and need. A product may ensure physical or emotional integrity (survival or health); it may give physical security (shelter, clothing, heat or food); or it may provide social security (communication, transport or education). Beyond this, a product may allow people to extend their own physical, spiritual, intellectual or other capabilities (for example, through the use of books or tools or other simple educational or recreational material). Or a product may provide for the refinement of human activity, and in doing so may use increasingly sophisticated but inessential approaches to the solution of basic needs.

Beyond this point, what counts is what people want, rather than what they need—and how much this counts depends of course on the extent to which a society will allow some members to indulge their desires while others have basic needs unfulfilled. We cannot suggest how such fundamental social issues be resolved—and to what extent they be resolved—by the influence of people as individuals, by people through government, or by business. But it does bear saying that, in a world in which millions die from the excesses of consumption while millions more die from malnutrition, real resolution is a long way off.

The *degree* of the benefit a product gives relates largely to the extent to which it improves on some earlier design or model—and to the cost of doing so. For example, a distinction could be made between products which:

—fill some vacuum through their unique effectiveness (such as a cure for a disease, a radio or a telephone)

—give some fundamental improvement over an existing class of products (for example, a transistor replacing a valve, a pneumatic tyre over a solid tyre)

—refine an existing function (such as a cartridge-loaded rather than bottle-fed pen)

—duplicate an existing function (as do countless 'me-too' products)

—disguise their essential sameness using more and less elaborate styling changes, often backed by aggressive marketing and promotional techniques (cars for example).

Finally, one might consider the *scope* of a benefit, and how widely that benefit might be felt. Does the product bring universal benefits (as may a drug like penicillin, or a bicycle); or selective benefits (a camera or an electric drill, for example); or exclusive or near-exclusive benefits (such as an ice-crusher, or a luxury car)? And what indirect (as well as direct) benefits are involved?

Another test could be applied in trying to assess the worth of a product. You could relate the nature, degree and scope of the benefit actually felt against the benefit that could be given.

You might question what could be made instead of a particular product, using the same resources, materials and expertise. The Old

Testament prophet Isaiah (Chapter 2, Verse 4) specifically recommended switching production from swords into ploughshares—and there would be parallels in other sectors of industry besides.

For example, a combine of trade unionists in the Lucas Aerospace group set out (in 1975–76) to prepare a 'Corporate Plan'[1] in an attempt both to safeguard employment in a vulnerable (defence-oriented) industry, and also to apply the skills of the existing work-force in the manufacture of socially useful and marketable 'alternative' products. The questionnaire they circulated to Lucas plants produced no fewer than 150 suggestions for the manufacture of alternative products, for which some basic but unsatisfied consumer need was believed to exist.

Another approach might be to establish what alternative applications and distribution might be found for existing products—and to what effect. For instance, it would be salutory at least to calculate how many deaths and how much disease caused directly by malnutrition could be eliminated by redistributing the nutritional equivalent of all pet food consumed in the West. (In the UK alone, dogs and cats are estimated to consume £350 millions worth of food each year (1975). Oxfam estimate there to be 500 million people suffering from malnutrition—and attribute 30 million deaths a year to malnutrition and related causes.)

Finally, one might question how existing products might be modified to give adequate or possibly improved performance, perhaps at lower cost—and also whether in the light of alternative priorities, certain products should exist at all.

There are many admirable examples of alternative technologies—of cases in which simple and appropriate means have been found to solve major problems, where conventional technologies have failed.[2] There are also numerous examples of the shortcomings of existing products (that is, a failure of technology or marketing, or both) in conventional situations. Take the car, for example:

—To stop people 'fiddling' car mileage readings, does one design and legislate for simple 'tamper-proof' odometers—or go to the seemingly extraordinary lengths of setting up computerised registers for recording individual car mileages, as a consortium of North of England local authorities has done?

—So long as private cars continue to be made and used (and it will not be for much longer on anything like the present scale) why clutter the dashboard with gadgets like map-reading lights or cigarette lighters—rather than install fundamentally useful equipment, such as a simple fuel consumption gauge?

—Since cars are regularly driven into each other, and into other obstacles, why allow the motor industry to sell cars with flashy, flimsy bumpers (often incorporating lights and other vulnerable parts) in particular, when even the height of these bumpers varies in different cars.

Further examples are given in later sections of this report.

Other benefits and costs

The worth of a product depends not only on its value to the consumer; it depends also on the costs and benefits associated with its manufacture and use. For example, poor conditions of work, high accident levels or environmental pollution may be characteristic of the product's manufacture, while the use of certain products may create accidents or ill-health, or waste-disposal problems.

Some production-related costs—or some measure of them, such as the market value of materials or labour—will be reflected in the price of the product, while others will not. Some costs—for example, the long-term health effects of a process material—may not be appreciated. Other costs—for instance, environmental pollution—may not be quantified or attributed to source. One reason for this is that information about such costs which is, or could be available, may never be disclosed.

Similarly, the price of a product will relate more to the benefits that the product is intended to give than to various unintended costs that may be associated with its use. A car, for instance, is intended to provide functional and recreational mobility, efficiency, convenience, excitement and so on. But the use of cars involves certain side-effects, as well:

Secondary effects on user	such as isolation, frustration, lack of exercise, expense, etc.
Secondary effects on others	such as pollution, noise, loss of amenity, etc.
Incidental effects	such as pressure on public transport systems, and for road building programmes, etc.
Effect of accidental use or misuse	such as personal injury and damage to property
Effect of waste	such as poor land use, litter and loss of amenity.

There are mechanisms for limiting or compensating for some of the costs involved in the production and use of different products. The two most obvious are bargaining by affected interests, and government control. Both, clearly, can be effective; equally, neither offers anything like a complete solution.

BARGAINING

In an ideal world, employees would all bargain for reasonable working conditions and equitable rates of pay, so that the production-related costs they might otherwise bear would ultimately be paid for by consumers.

In practice though, the bargaining powers of employees may be exceptionally strong (coal miners or senior civil servants, for example) or they may be virtually non-existent (homeworkers, for example). Moreover, most employees have no *absolute* rights to rewarding work, to a safe working environment, to a reasonable pension or even to the 'rate for the job'. They may bargain only for the best conditions that may be provided in a competitive environment—and these do not relate so much to any acceptable minimum·standard, as to the *lowest standards* which any significant competitor can impose on its employees, or otherwise persuade them to accept.[3]

However, many employees are usually far better placed to bargain than other stakeholders affected by what businesses do. The impotence of these interests is underlined by the means of protest they use (for example, demonstrations by the polluted); and also by the occasional activities of investors or consumers who intervene in cases where the injured parties are not able to protect themselves. Examples include boycotts or demonstrations over racial or ethnic discrimination, the overexploitation of endangered species, inhumane working conditions, and the question of compensation for 'Thalidomide children'.

GOVERNMENT CONTROL

Governments may limit or offset various production and use-related costs by controlling the design or distribution of products, by regulating production, by providing financial incentives or compensations, and through taxation. Government may be better placed than any other single interest both to detect social damage and to estimate its significance in relation to benefit; and also to contain or compensate for such damage as may be done.

In practice, though, the effectiveness of government intervention is limited. For one thing, a democratic government would be highly unlikely to have the power to apportion benefit and cost as it saw fit— and it probably would not be a democratic government if it did. All government can do is to bargain and, inevitably, it bargains least effectively with opposing interests having the greatest power.

In addition, the quality of government intervention is limited by the fact that government acts itself as a vested interest. Government has its own objectives, and its own need for power which allows it to pursue its purpose. Governments take power which allow them to make war or peace; to be partial, opportunistic or ruthless. And all governments take power to prevent their being seen to fail. The extensive abuse of secrecy in government is just one example which clearly distinguishes between government purpose on the one hand, and public purpose on the other.

So what is a product worth?

So what is a product worth? Is chalk actually 'worth' more than cheese —and if so what should be done about it?

The first thing to be said is that chalk and cheese are simply what people accept them for. This is not necessarily what they are and—in the absence of information about what they *really* are—could never be so.

Much of this information is now missing. Any discussion about the real qualities of chalk or cheese is effectively stifled by those who have information which others do not; and by those who deluge the discussion with their views and their views alone. But the issue ultimately is not whether chalk is worth more or less than cheese—but whether anyone *cares* what either is worth. A totally uncaring approach to this question of the 'worth' of a product is a mark of aimlessness in society— just as a string of aimless products is in some measure an indicator of society's own lack of worth.

Suitability for purpose

The potential of a product can be realised only when the designer identifies user and other requirements and then adequately interprets them.

In *Design for the Real World*, Victor Papanek suggests that 'there is much that is designed well, incredibly much more that is designed badly and a frightening amount of things that are never designed at all'[4]. Papanek's criticism is directed partly at products which, in the light of 'real world' priorities, should not be designed at all. But it clearly also applies to products which are, or should be, designed to meet substantial needs—but which actually do not. There are countless examples of these, many obvious to people without formal training in design. The following (which have nothing to do with Papanek) relate to road vehicles:

—Most bicycles have caliper brakes whose blocks rub helplessly in wet weather against the smooth stylish chromium-plated rim of the wheel. Over 20 years ago, the governments' Transport and Road Research Laboratory reported that braking performance in wet weather could be improved about 20 per cent with unplated rims. With hub brakes, the efficiency and safety could be improved a good deal more.[5]

—The forks on many motorcycles allow dangerous juddering in the front wheel—the 'tank slappers', so called. A solution proposed in 1976 by a Manchester University design team was reportedly rejected by major motorcycle manufacturers—despite the fact it was cheaper, and effective—on the grounds that customers would not buy it, because the design was not 'sexy' enough.[6]

—The design of the government's three-wheeler invalid carriage is notorious for its failings in safety, comfort and convenience. Baroness Sharp, who chaired an official enquiry into the provision and use of these machines, has commented: 'I do not think there is any real doubt that the trike is dangerous . . . Whether, as some would claim, it is the most lethal car on the road, I do not know; but I think it is getting on that way. . . '[7]

—A government committee[8] has estimated that 'the life of car bodies could be extended by a period of two to three years, merely by the avoidance of moisture traps in the design and by giving suitable advice in the driver's handbook on control and prevention of corrosion'.

—The problem of wind resistance has apparently been largely over-looked in the design of most heavy goods vehicles, towed trailers and caravans. A solution to this problem could bring substantial reductions in fuel consumption, and also reduce noise.[9]

Most of these problems arise not because designers have failed to appreciate the first principles, but because they have failed to stick to them. First principles supposedly dictate that designers design what people need and want. This is a considerable responsibility, and one which offers so much scope for unintentional failure as to obviate the need for deliberate abuse.

Interpreting consumer needs

The way in which a designer interprets user and other requirements will be influenced by a variety of constraints—the most important probably being cost. The designer would be very unlikely to have—and very unlikely actually to need—the freedom to design to a maximum quality (that is, 'money no object'). He or she would normally design to an 'optimum' quality—a level of quality which can be achieved, for instance, by:

—Designing to or within certain cost limits (in other words, getting the maximum benefit possible at a given cost).

—Designing up to an estimated point of diminishing return (that is creating a product which gave maximum usable value for money).

—Designing for an 'economic' level of failure (that is, by balancing the cost of achieving a particular quality in *all* products against the cost of not doing so in some).

Which compromise is chosen is critically important. For example, the decision to build within a particular cost limit may lead to the design of a product which gives poor value (this is otherwise known as bringing rotten products within the reach of less well-off consumers). Similarly, if balancing the cost of failure involves assessing costs felt by manufacturers, rather than of the (possibly far higher) costs felt by consumers, the results may be disastrous. Thus, if all accidents actually attributable to tyre failure were identifiable as such, which they are not,[10] then manufacturers would be bound to recalculate what they now estimate to be the economic cost of failure *to them*, in order to meet their full liability.

The compromises made in interpreting design requirements need not relate to straightforward external constraints on cost. Many constraints are self-imposed.

As earlier examples suggest, designers and manufacturers between them are quite capable of sacrificing safety or efficiency—when by doing so they think they can make products seemingly more attractive to buy. Equally, obsolescence may be built into a product (or not designed out) when this fits a marketing strategy which involves the constant revamping of products, so as to always have something 'new', and 'more' of that something, to sell. This happens frequently and with many products—and above all it happens with American cars. The US Labor Department, for example, has estimated that the value of 'quality changes' in 1977 auto models were worth an average $47.05 at factory prices ($59.15 retail) although the average manufacturers' recommended retail prices were increased by $382.30.[11]

These examples are important not only because they indicate very questionable priorities in design—but also because they suggest that designers have considerable freedom to abuse their trust. The presumptions they make that consumers are willing to pay more for apparent improvements—and the presumed unwillingness of consumers to pay extra for real improvements—should also be wide open to question.

There are underlying questions as well: what steps have been taken to identify consumer and other requirements? What research, testing and analysis has been carried out, and to what effect? Has the emphasis in such enquiries been on finding out what consumers will *buy*, or on finding out what they and others may *need*, or simply on establishing how many more 'me-too' products the market may bear?

Some of these questions may be anticipated or answered in various product specifications. These are statements[12] which embody and formally define the ideas that designers, among others, have about the products they create. They may indicate both the extent to which user requirements have been understood and the ways in which they have been interpreted.

When major corporate consumers buy products, they will generally buy to a specification. When Marks and Spencer buys clothes, or Tesco buys baked beans, or British Leyland buys tyres, or a government department buys office equipment—they buy to a specification. They may have their own specification, they may use the manufacturer's, or they may refer to a generally accepted standard—but, in any case, their purchasing power allows them to know, at least in theory, what they are getting.[13]

Materials, mechanics and aesthetics

At least a specification defines what it is intended that consumers should get. What they actually get is at best as good as what they were intended to get—but it may very well be worse.

Materials

A product design specification determines what materials are used, what form they take and how they are put together. These three things determine what a product is and does, and what it looks like. They should also *be* determined by what the product should be: design and performance should be related, as chicken is to egg.

The designer's choice of materials would be governed by several different factors. These include:

—the availability, supply, consistency and cost of the materials that might be used;
—the properties of these materials (such as weight, toxicity, strength, etc.) and their appearance;
—their suitability over alternatives, but also their replaceability by alternatives;
—the requirements for a manufacturing process;
—the conditions in which the materials may be used, manufactured, handled, prepared, installed, serviced or maintained, etc;
—the effect of the environment on these materials (like temperature, pressure, shock, humidity, etc. and any combination thereof)—and

also the impact of these materials on the environment in which they are used.

Though there are fairly well-established procedures for specifying different materials in different situations—in practice, they may be overlooked or ignored, sometimes with disastrous results. The most obvious and typical failures include:

—Deliberately over-emphasising in the design qualities which make a product worth selling, rather than worth buying—such as using a cheap or flashy material and thereby downgrading function. There are numerous examples of this—the use of cheap, flimsy plastics in refrigerators, or of colouring and flavouring added to baby food for the benefit of mother (who buys and samples the food) rather than child.

—Overlooking consumer requirements—probably through neglect, rather than design. This could result from a failure to take due account of evidence of persistent defects in a product—or of, say, the unexpectedly high movement of certain spare parts through stores. Equally, there could be neglect in analysing the cause and effects of accidents involving (among others) the product, or of premature and 'natural' product failures.

—Overlooking other requirements. In particular, the use of new materials, or combinations of materials, may be associated with unintended and unforeseen consequences, especially for non-users (who are 'compulsory consumers') and on the physical environment. The use of fluorocarbons in aerosol sprays is a case in point.

—Failure to appreciate the availability and suitability of alternative materials and/or an unwillingness to use them. The use of improved materials may be avoided for any or all of the three reasons given above—or simply because knowledge of the existence of a new material, or experience and capacity to handle a new technology, is absent.

—Failure to ensure that, in practice, the right materials are used— for example by failing to specify tests on incoming materials to check their conformity with the standard required; or by failing to specify that materials be appropriately labelled or identified, so as to avoid the wrong materials being used in a manufacturing or related process.

Mechanics

Essentially the same factors determine what a designer makes of the 'mechanics'—in other words the form of the materials used and the relationship between them.

Two things in particular stand out as bad and fairly widespread practice. One is making design changes essentially for the sake of change. The habit is exemplified by 'innovation' in the detergent industry which, according to the Monopolies Commission report of 1966, amounted largely to 'changing the formulation of existing products for the sake of "improvements" which are of little or no intrinsic value to the user'.[14]

Secondly, there may be failure to use standard parts where these can be used—and, worse still, failure to carry forward the same standard parts from one product model to the next. The use of standard and well-tried parts and sub-assemblies not only reduces the chances of product failure; it is also likely to be much cheaper, and makes repair and replacement quicker and easier too. At the other extreme, the failure to use standard or at least comparable parts from one model of a product to the next forces waste and obsolescence through lack of available spares. For example, a 1974 study by the Center for Policy Alternatives at the Massachusetts Institute of Technology reported:

> In the refrigerator service business, the major problem noted by servicemen was the lack of parts' standardisation, which forces them to maintain larger (spares) inventories. However, the servicemen also explained that most customers faced with major repairs prefer to discard their old refrigerators and purchase new ones.[15]

This report did not question whether the preference of 'most customers faced with major repairs' was influenced either by sales pressure, or by the lack of spares with which to carry out repairs. If UK and US experience are comparable, it almost certainly was: for, in the first three months of 1976 alone, the Office of Fair Trading recorded over 600 complaints about shortages of spare parts.[16]

Aesthetics

However, there is (or was) supposed to be some difference between the preferences of US and UK consumers for styling. It has been suggested that one of the main reasons why the UK 'appliance manufacturer has tended towards conformity in the styling of his products' is that the British public has a 'deep-rooted aversion from the American practice of "planned obsolescence" . . . '[17]

This may or may not be the case today—as it was said to be in 1966. In any case, a social audit would not be concerned with the question of conformity as such—but mainly about:

(1) The significance and frequency of styling changes—and any

evidence to suggest that such changes have been required, if not welcomed, by consumers, rather than thrust upon them.

(2) The relationship between 'function' and 'form'. Consumers are entitled to expect from designers at least that form will be compatible with function. Function should certainly never be subordinated to form—as it is in the case of, say, mud and rust traps, disguised as muscle-bound wheel-arches, in some cars.

(3) The cost of styling. Styling has to be paid for by consumers in capital, running and replacement costs. Consumers' willingness to pay for flash or frills in a design should not be presumed—at least so long as consumers are never actually told how much they do pay.

Checklist on design

The following questions are intended both to summarise and amplify the main issues raised in the preceding chapter. They should be used in conjunction with the general questions relating to policy, organisation, procedures, resources and effects listed in Chapter 3 (pages 27 to 36); and also with the list of standards identified in Chapter 2 (pages 17 to 25).

Purpose and value of design

(1) What are the principal benefits and costs associated with the product's manufacture and use?

(2) Who enjoys these benefits, and who pays the costs?

(3) How do such costs and benefits compare with the costs and benefits that would be involved using modified designs, alternative technologies or the same technologies to different ends?

Comments

These three questions, which summarise a number of points made in the text about the purpose of design, are included not because there are any right or wrong answers, or any simple yardsticks by which to distinguish the 'responsible' producer from any other. They are there to prompt readers *not* to take for granted that products deserve to exist simply because there are consumers who will buy them and producers who will make them. (Equally, there may be products and services which should exist, even when and if they cannot pay their way).

In suggesting that different products have different (positive and negative) social value, there is of course an implied threat to the freedom of choice in the marketplace that now exists. However, what really threatens this freedom is its abuse—by producers who fob off consumers with mutton dressed as lamb, and by a minority of consumers whose overindulgence gives positive incitement to feelings of revulsion or revolt. For all this, freedom of choice is something well worth preserving—not so much for the choice, as for the freedom from any authority which might seek to curb it.

Nature of research and development work

(4) What research and development work goes into the making of new or modified products; and what is the real significance of any changes made (or not made) as a result?

(5) What is the strategic intent behind the company's research and development work? Is the company making changes largely for the sake of change, or making real and radical improvements; is it responding to market pressures or setting out to find or force new market openings; is it trying to find ways of making products more economically or with cheaper, better or safer materials; and is it making things that people need, or merely things that people can be persuaded to buy?

(6) What research and survey work is done into the attitudes and experiences of past, present and prospective product users—including users of ageing and secondhand products? And what have been the causes and effects of such enquiries?

(7) What testing and development work is done? What tests and examinations are made of suppliers' and competitors' products—and on the company's own products in their prototype, new, used and failed conditions?

(8) What testing has been directed towards eliminating design failures—and in making improvements (for example in the safety, reliability, durability or economy of products)? And how has such work in fact influenced the product design?

(9) What analyses are done—for example of customer complaints, service returns, the movement of spare and replacement parts through stores, or of work done under guarantee? And what effect has all this activity had, both in correcting defects and in making positive improvements in the product design?

(10) What possible unforeseen or unintended effects might be associated with the design or modification of the company's products? (*Remember fridge doors*). What indications are there that the company has looked exhaustively for evidence of such effects, and taken appropriate action to remedy harmful ones?

Comments

The object here is to question both the commitment and competence of the company. Evidence of the company's commitment or intent may be found, for example, in its decisions to make or not to make particular products or improvements; or in the way in which it does research into consumer preference or need. Again, there are no simple standards by which to judge commitment of one kind or another— unless the company has set standards for itself, or unless the question of negligence or incompetence arises.

Access to survey, research, testing and development work may be difficult to obtain. Some of the data is sensitive and likely to be considered confidential by most companies. However, if the results of such research are considered confidential, there is no obvious reason why the company should not make known the questions to which it has been seeking answers. Ask for blank questionnaires and enquire also about the titles of any research and development reports that have been commissioned or produced.

Design fitness for purpose

(11)   Do formal design specifications exist for each of the company's products, and for the components used in them?

(12)   How comprehensive do such specifications appear to be, and do they comply fully with the provisions of the British Standards 'Guide to the Preparation of Specifications'? (This guide, Ref. PD 6112 which was published in May 1967, is only an outline guide, it may nevertheless be useful as such.)

(13)   How does the design of the product compare with previous designs, rejected designs, competitors' designs, with the simplest functional design, and with the best and best practicable designs?

(14)   What patents are there which relate to the design in question? Do these suggest significant user requirements which may or may not have been met; or point to the possibility of making better designs, or making the same design in a better way?

(15)   For whom have the company's products been made, and what influence would this have on the adoption or rejection of certain designs?

Comments

The implications of questions (11) to (14) will be fairly clear, but the point raised in the last question deserves some comment.

Remember that from the design/sales point of view, the consumer is the purchaser—but not necessarily the user—of the product. The distinction is critical because:

—The purchaser may be an institution, and institutions do not buy like aggregations of consumers. Take two examples: the Department of Health and Social Security purchasing three-wheeler invalid cars; and Marks and Spencer buying pyjamas. The DHSS's acceptance or choice of the (previously mentioned) appallingly designed three-wheeler for disabled people demonstrates among many other things how the needs and priorities of buyer and user may totally differ. By contrast Marks and Spencer has to sell the pyjamas it buys—and the fact that it dominates this glamorous market suggests that it does not face insuperable difficulties in doing so. But Marks and Spencer, in its onward march for efficiency, caters to majority demand and prefers to stick to simple stocking and ordering procedures. It therefore only buys pyjamas with elastic rather than cord at the waist—and, because of its dominance as a buyer in the pyjama market, it is said now to be very hard indeed to find pyjamas with cords anywhere.

—The purchaser may sell the product long before the end of its useful (or potentially useful) life, and this may greatly influence the manufacturers' approach to the design. For example, most cars in the UK are sold to fleet buyers, most of whom sell their cars and replace them with new ones at least every two years. For this reason, manufacturers are not particularly interested in the performance of older cars, or in building cars to last—unlike those who actually use these cars for most of the vehicles' lives.

Design standards

(16) What standards affect product design?

(17) To what extent are these standards effectively enforced—and would the likelihood of non-detection or non-prosecution be likely to affect the design?

(18) What would be the likely consequences for the company of failing to achieve good standards of design?

Comments

Bear in mind that standards (of the kind described in Chapter 2, pages 17 to 25) need not dictate design, but may nevertheless affect it. For instance, the legal requirement to have a 1 mm minimum depth on the tread of a care tyre applies to the motorist rather than to the designer. Still, the requirement is relevant to the design of new car tyres, in that the design may be improved by building a tread wear indicator into the tyre (see *Social Audit on Avon* pp. 56–7).

The influence of formal or other standards on design depends not only on 'formal' enforcement. The quality of design may be influenced by the likelihood of the manufacturer having to assume liability in the case of design failure; or by the possibility of critical comment following product tests or evaluations.

Another factor is how much information the manufacturer has to disclose about the design of his products. In this context, it is likely that an outrageous deception carried out by the cosmetics people Max Factor was facilitated by the absence of any requirement for ingredient labelling of cosmetics. In 1974, Max Factor were pro-secuted and fined (minimally) for making misleading statements about their Swedish Formula make-up—which they had claimed in their advertising was 'screened for any possible irritants' and from which they said they had sifted out 'any irritants that could cause rashes, blotches and other serious reactions'. Following complaints of serious reactions, it was found that out of the 15 ingredients (in the range of six preparations) eight were known irritants, and two were possibly so (*Chemist and Druggist* (20 July, 1974)).

Justification of design

(19) What indications are given—for example, in the content of the instructions, the terms of any guarantee, or the emphasis in the advertising—of any limitations in the design?

(20) What justification can be given for the inclusion of each of the major features of the design, taking into account function and efficiency, cost and appeal—and would consumers be likely to be willing to pay for these if (a) they knew exactly what they would and would not get from the design; and (b) they knew how much they were paying for it?

Comments

This last question sums up the whole question of product design as it affects the consumer. It suggests a standard for judging design quality which should be perfectly acceptable to any producer confident of the value of his products. It further suggests that a manufacturer who cannot or will not justify the design of his products, in response to a reasonable request to do so, is in effect failing to provide evidence of his right to do business with consumers.

The power that a manufacturer now has to attempt to sell to consumers, by fair means or foul, is simply in the nature of a privilege. It should not be overextended. The right to sell should be earned.

5 Manufacture and Quality Control

Last night I heard one of the guys say we did 391 cars. How many welds are we supposed to put in a car? They have governmental regulations for consumer protection. We just put what we think ought to be put in there and then let it go (laughs). There are specifications which we pay very little attention to . . . You have inspectors who are supposed to check every kind of defect. All of us know those things don't get corrected . . . Whenever we make a mistake, we always say, 'Don't worry about it, some dingaling'll buy it.' (Laughs).[1]

The Contractor shall ensure that manufacturing operations are carried out under controlled conditions. Controlled conditions include documented work instructions defining the manner of manufacturing or processing and including criteria for workmanship, suitable manufacturing equipment and any special working environment. Workmanship shall be defined to the greatest practical extent by written standards, or samples inspected by the Contractor and the Quality Assurance Representative as examples of satisfactory workmanship . . .[2]

It is hardly fair to take the spot welder's remarks out of context simply to confirm what every consumer must know and deplore. For in the full context—which describes the spot welder's soul-destroying work routines—it becomes so much clearer why defects get through. But the point here is only that they may, or do.

The second quote says defects should not get through, and does so in terms which virtually suggest they cannot. But this quote is mainly interesting because it underlines the right that *corporate* consumers have—and use—to find out how their products are being made. This standard, produced by the Ministry of Defence, says that manufacturers should 'be prepared to substantiate by objective evidence that they have maintained full control over their manufacturing operations and have performed inspections which demonstrate the acceptability of the product'.[3]

61

Finally, the contrast between the quotes suggests the major practical limitations there may be in ensuring that manufacture involves the faithful execution of design. And this, in turn, explains why the emphasis in this chapter is on quality control, rather than anything else.

What determines quality?

Some of the main quality 'factors' have been identified (in the form of suggested production requirements) by the US Consumer Product Safety Commission.[4] They refer specifically to product safety, but apply equally to quality of any kind:

(1) *Materials.* Raw, semi-finished or finished materials must conform to configurations and conditions specified during product design (this requirement holds also for suppliers' materials). For those materials modified or degraded by handling, storage and/or processing during production, periodic verification is necessary to assure that prescribed materials are being used. In this regard, it is necessary that materials be identified and labelled . . . to prevent mistaken utilisation.

(2) *Work instructions.* Except work operations that are so simple as to render guidance unnecessary, operations affecting safety are to be described in writing, including inspection and testing procedures. These work instructions may exist in many forms including work orders, operation sheets, inspection logs, repair logs, test procedures and process specifications. They may also specify (a) equipment to be used for particular operations, (b) traceability arrangements identifying the person(s) who performed each of the operations, and (c) forms for recording quantitative data such as test readings and dates accomplished.

(3) *Facilities.* Differing products, designs and fabrication processes necessitate varied levels of precision and accuracy of manufacturing equipment and tooling. The precision and accuracy of equipment and tooling must be commensurate with product requirements, that is, equipment capable of consistently fabricating products to established tolerances.

(4) *Production processes.* Production processes (for example, welding, soldering, heat-treating, bonding) generate product characteristics, whose acceptability is difficult to evaluate. To minimise the probability that these operations are resulting in hazardous defects, it is necessary to institute controls of equipment, methods and qualifications of personnel. Such controls consist of scheduled

inspections of equipment, surveillance of compliance with procedures, and verification of competance of personnel. Records of the results of such inspection and surveillance are necessary to substantiate the state of control of these processes.

(5) *Repair.* When a manufactured product is determined to be potentially hazardous, it may be discarded or repaired. In the event that the product is repaired, necessary operations must be monitored to the same degree or more intensively than original production operations. For example, when it is determined that a component is unsafe, adequate precautions, including testing as required, must be taken to assure that the replacement component is effective in eliminating the product hazard identified. Repair may require more skilled operators, more precise equipment and more closely controlled materials. Repair operations performed by distributors or other representatives of the manufacturers must be subject to the same controls as would apply to products repaired in the production facility. As with original production, repair practices are to be described in work instructions.

(6) *Work environment.* The fabrication of safe and reliable products is a function of many factors, including physical working conditions. A satisfactory working and processing environment (for example, good lighting and controlled temperature and humidity) are necessary prerequisites for the manufacture of safe products.

(7) *Handling and storage.* Raw and manufactured materials used in production are to be handled, packaged and stored under conditions that preclude damage and resultant safety hazards. For example, items such as special adhesives which have limited shelf-life and require prescribed storage conditions must be identified in terms of their shelf-life limitations and should be monitored by periodic inspections to assure their continued effectiveness and safety. Precautions for handling, packaging and storage are normally prescribed in work instructions.

It is one thing to quote such requirements, and another to make them work. From a distance, from the perspective of the consumer, it might seem that you can get what you want simply by piling on requirements and controls. However, what may be control over processes or machines, amounts to discipline for the people who work them. And, beyond the point at which discipline becomes unacceptable, it does not effectively work.

There is no need to discuss the need for control of error by attending to some of the most obvious natural and human causes of it. But it is worth saying first that such issues should not be overlooked in a social audit, and secondly, that informal enquiry of the kind done by Studs Terkel (see reference [1]) may be of greater value than more conventional methods—in identifying the kind of failures which occur in manufacture, as well as their cause.

Quality Control

The terms 'quality control', 'quality assurance' or 'product assurance' refer to everything and anything deliberately done to ensure that manufactured products conform to both design and user requirements. Quality control is not simply an afterthought in production. It is, or should be, a comprehensive system for preventing all failures, at any stage—whether in design, production, purchasing of materials, packaging, distribution, or any other function in manufacture.

There can be no question of making any detailed review: there are simply too many ways in which quality control functions may be organised and assigned, and too great a range of activities and applications involved. However, there are a few particularly important elements which should be mentioned—because they are fundamental to the effective operation of any quality control system. They include:

(1) *Inspection, measurement and testing.* It is the manufacturer's responsibility to arrange for appropriate examinations to be made of any critical elements in a production system, to compare requirements with actual results. Examinations may be required of production techniques and equipment—as well as of raw or processed materials, components and assemblies, and part-produced and completed products. Examinations of products and equipment should be significant, objective, exact and uniform. They should be carried out at each stage beyond which no proper (or economic) inspection can be made; and should include a final inspection which provides, or reviews, complete evidence of full conformity with requirements.

(2) *Documentation and records.* All design, production and related requirements, and work instructions, should be fully documented. All changes should be recorded, and provisions made for the prompt removal of all obsolete documents from all points of issue and use. Records should be maintained to demonstrate the effective operation of all quality control functions.

(3) *Statistical methods.* Appropriate techniques and procedures should be used for all calibration, measurement and sampling involved in effecting quality control.

(4) *Corrective actions.* Quality control systems should include procedures for the detection and correction of any element which may lead to the production of substandard materials. These procedures should provide for continuing analysis both of rejected or

reworked materials, to determine the cause of failure and the corrective action needed; and of all production operations which do or may cause substandard products to be made. It is essential also that provisions are made to identify and segregate non-conforming material, to prevent any possibility of misappropriation or misuse.

Quality assurance standards along these lines have been developed largely on the initiative of public purchasing agencies (and notably the Procurement Executive of the Ministry of Defence) whose commercial muscle has allowed them to insist on the terms on which they do business. In the UK, the Ministry of Defence has approved the quality assurance arrangements of over 2000 firms (between 1972–76). There is no legal requirement for approval—but firms without it are highly unlikely to be invited to tender for business.

In the open market, there is not only no requirement, but also no specific incentive, for a firm to maintain a standard level of quality control. The standards that are actually observed are determined almost entirely by the firms themselves—that is by both their capability and motivation. Capability involves both knowing what to do, and having the resources to do it. Motivation depends on the consequences for the firm of producing to, or below, a particular quality—and, above all, on consumers' ability to *detect* variation in quality. Their ability or inability, in turn, may be influenced by several interrelated factors. These include:

—What consumers may be persuaded to believe about a quality, or about the importance of a particular quality.
—Lack of information—resulting, for example, from the absence of aggregated data about product performance; or from difficulty in relating cause (substandard quality) to effect (malfunction).[5]
—Simple inability to detect significant variation in quality—for example, the nutritional value of drink or food. (The market research technique known as 'discrimination testing' has reportedly been developed as a means of exploring and exploiting this 'failure' to detect quality variation.)[6]

It is impossible to generalise about the standards of quality control actually observed in different industries. However, the evidence from specific cases is not encouraging. In 1972, for example, Aird[7] reported that: '*Motoring Which?*, which has now tested over 200 cars, bought anonymously from ordinary garages as if by an ordinary private motorist, has not yet found one to be delivered without faults.' He goes on to argue convincingly (though not conclusively) that 'poor workmanship and inadequate inspection is also much cheaper for the manufacturer than the cost of a good job well done'.

Quality assurance schemes

In the circumstances, one must question whether quality assurance standards of the kind required by major purchasing agencies can and should be applied across the board.

There is considerable evidence that such standards would be cost-effective if applied—though the precise costs and benefits would be hard to assess. The 1971 report of the government Committee on the Means of Authenticating the Quality of Engineering Products and Materials concluded: 'we are convinced that the value of such benefit would exceed by many times the costs involved'. The cost of the 'independent quality surveillance service' they proposed was estimated at 'probably not more than one per cent of the purchase price' of the goods covered by the service—and this was suggested to be substantially less than the possible savings involved:

> The savings that can be achieved are illustrated in the reports provided by individual companies following Quality and Reliability Year (1966–67) some of which registered savings of 4 per cent of turnover and more. Whilst undoubtedly some of these companies commenced with excessive quality costs, well managed companies also showed substantial reductions as a result of a critical approach to their methods of quality control and analysis of quality costs.[8]

This Committee was concerned specifically about quality assurance for the public sector—which was estimated to purchase about 40 per cent of the output of all engineering products. So, had its proposals been acted on—and they were not—this would not have directly affected the quality of goods supplied elsewhere. However, there have since been proposals for similar but extended schemes—and notably for a service which would involve the licensing of individual firms, which would then be allowed to display (that is, advertise) a 'quality mark' of approval.[9]

There is no obvious reason why such schemes could not work; but many reasons why they should.

Checklist on Manufacture and Quality Control

The following questions are intended both to summarise and amplify the main issues raised in the preceding chapter. They should be used in conjunction with the general questions relating to policy, organisation, procedures, resources and effects listed in Chapter 3 (pages 27 to 36); and also with the list of standards identified in Chapter 2 (pages 17 to 25).

Appropriateness of standards adopted

(1) What standards are applied—or implied by the procedures actually used—in the manufacture and quality control process?

(2) Is the company consistent in the standards it observes?

Comments

Standards relating specifically to manufacture and quality control have been produced by the US Department of Defence, the US Consumer Product Safety Commission, the North Atlantic Treaty Organisation, the UK Ministry of Defence and the British Standards Institution—among several other authorities. The standards used by the Procurement Executive of the Ministry of Defence are particularly useful because (like their NATO counterparts) they list requirements for three different levels of quality control and inspection systems. In descending order of rigour, these are:

Quality Control System Requirements for Industry (DEF-STAN 05–21)

Inspection System Requirements for Industry (DEF-STAN 05–24)

Basic Inspection Requirements for Industry (DEF-STAN 05–29)

In addition, the Ministry of Defence has issued associated guides, to help simplify the interpretation and use of these standards. For instance, DEF-STAN 05–22 is a 'Guide for the Evaluation of a Contractors' Quality Control System for Compliance with DEF-STAN 05–21'—the first of the three standards listed above. These standards appear well suited for use in a social audit.

However, evidence of actual compliance with these and similar standards, which may be required of particular firms by public purchasing authorities, cannot usually be obtained. The Ministry of Defence will identify firms which have satisfied its requirements and which are included on its approved list of contractors—but individual inspection reports are not made public. Inclusion on this list may not be particularly significant—in that not all firms do or will undertake 'defence' contracts; and the approvals given to those who do relate only to the public sector contracting side of the business, which may be quite separate from any other.

The question about the company's consistency in its standards refers to the standards applied in all aspects of its business. The significance of consistency is acknowledged in many formal inspection procedures. In evaluating manufacturing standards, the standards relating to employee welfare, conditions of work, and industrial relations would be particularly relevant.

When examining the manufacturing standards themselves, it may be useful to establish whether the same or different standards are followed in fulfilling different orders for basically the same product. For example, cars are said to be produced to several different standards: one for ordinary domestic markets, another for exports, and another for 'specials'—that is, for motoring correspondents or VIPs. The use of different procedures might indicate known areas of weakness, and the adequacy of measures used to remedy them.

Effectiveness of standards

(3) What evidence of the success or failure of the adopted standards is given, for example, by:

—the levels of, and variations in, recorded failure and success rates?
—the working of arrangements and agreements between the company and employees (and their representatives) as these affect such things as targets for quality or quantity of output, discipline and methods and conditions of work?
—the incidence and nature of consumer complaints, whether reported or unreported, explained or unexplained?
—indirect indications, such as service and repair data, turnover of spares, warranty bills, insurance premiums and terms, etc.?

(4) What evidence of commitment to standards is given, for example, by:

—the use of audit and related procedures designed to detect failures or make improvements?
—the actions taken when failures occur, both to correct mistakes and to prevent their recurrence?

Comments

Manufacture can be thought of as a process of trial and error; quality control as a process to contain error to an appropriate low. A social audit should concentrate first, on seeing that the quality control system is designed to detect and eliminate errors to a low enough level—taking into account the consequences of failing to do so. (The consequences of a 0.1 per cent failure rate in the manufacture of cheap ballpoint pens are clearly very different from the same level of failure in, say, fire extinguishers.)

Secondly, a social audit should establish that the quality control system has been made and allowed to operate in the intended manner

—and should seek evidence of this by examining all major data on failures which have occurred (whether detected in or beyond the factory) and establishing what, if any, corrective action has been taken.

The procedures for doing this have been outlined in the previously mentioned lists of requirements, and guides on their interpretation, published by the Ministry of Defence.

6 Packaging and Labelling

Though there is a clear distinction between 'packaging' and 'labelling', we have lumped them together as one, because they overlap in two major functions: protection and display. In this chapter, we are concerned with both of these, and also with the monetary and ecological costs of packaging waste.

Protection includes both protecting the product and protecting the consumer. For protection of the product, requirements for the design and manufacture of the package are exactly the same as for the product itself. The package should be functional and economical—whatever else it may be—and should be designed and made to conform strictly with the requirements of producer and consumer alike. Its purpose is to sustain the product—during manufacture, handling and storage, at the point of sale, and ultimately to the point at which the product is to be used, perhaps until the end of its useful life.

Packaging may protect the consumer, by indicating what the product is and what it is for; what and how much the product contains, and what it costs; how the product should or should not be used; the terms on which the product is sold; and by whom and when the product was made.

Display, which may influence the style, content and form of the package, is an integral part of all this. It may affect the way in which the product is protected but, more important, it may help or hinder consumers to get what they believe they are getting, or to get what they actually need or want. Such help or hindrance comes in three main guises, all explained by the fact that the purpose of display is to sell.

At its most aggressive, selling through display involves imposing on the consumer not to *not* buy. For example—many smallish items are sold only in quantity (such as a pair of pedals or mudguards for a bike, or a dozen wood screws) and consumers may be forced to buy more than they require, and at disproportionate extra expense.[1] Similarly, a display may persuade consumers to buy on impulse products which, before setting eyes on them, they had not consciously decided to acquire. Evidence of purchasing behaviour in supermarkets suggests that consumers emerged, on average, with 45 per cent more purchases than they had decided to make before entering.[2]

At another level, packaging display may merely 'help' the consumer to *want* to buy. The element of appeal may be so obvious as to defy the consumer to overlook it—or it may be totally surreptitious. The perceived size of a container can, for instance, be varied significantly by changing the colour, style and size of the label. Equally, a packet may not convey, or may de-emphasise, information about the quality or safety of the product which might deter consumers from buying. It will exaggerate any positive and persuasive 'information' instead.

And, finally, the display may actually help the consumer by honestly representing the product for what it is, or will in fact be, to the consumer—rather than for what it might conceivably be in the consumer's hopes or dreams. This is clearly true of own-brand displays more than others: the 'promise' is in the quality and the price, rather than in the clouds or elsewhere.

Information

This is not to suggest that all purchasing decisions by consumers should be made on a totally premeditated and rational basis—even if consumers should have enough information to allow them to do so, if they want. Nor is it automatically unacceptable to emphasise the immaterial qualities in a brand or product—provided sufficient hard information is also given. Consumers should at least be allowed to appreciate the basis and also the cost of the deliverance they may be offered through the use of a particular brand of, say, soap powder, eyewash, or baked beans.

There is clearly a balance to be struck between reason, on the one hand, and something like fun, on the other. But the question is not so much *where* this balance should be as *who* should determine it, and how.

The question 'who?' is almost rhetorical—seeing as it is the consumer who ends up with and pays for either value and/or fun. But, apart from this, the typical producer's underlying motives should disqualify him at least from having the power to decide what information consumers should *not* be given.

The reason for this is not wholly unconnected with the reasons for which producers were disqualified by law, some 40 years ago, for selling caustics for the 'cure of cancer, without the knife'.[3] For, whatever the law may have changed, it has not radically changed the motives of those who sold cancer 'cures' then and cold 'cures' today. If you doubt this, you have only to contemplate what would surely happen if the law relating to weights, measures and trade descriptions were repealed tomorrow.

Having said this, the question who should decide what information consumers should have, and how, is not as straightforward as it might seem.

For a start, a decision has to be made about priorities in information. Some information—for example, about the unit price, or weight of a product—will have universal relevance and always be welcome. On the other hand, the potential use of some information may not always be generally appreciated. For example, the relevance of 'nutritional labelling' or 'energy efficiency' will probably be more apparent to those familiar with *aggregated* evidence of nutritional deficiency or energy waste, than to many individual consumers of empty foods or inefficient products.

More to the point, some information of this kind may be positively resented. To take an unusual example, you might think it absurd to suggest a requirement for the safety-labelling of bunk-beds—certainly before (and perhaps even after) knowing that, in the US, around 13 500 children each year require hospital treatment, after falling out of them.[4] But even if you are convinced of the case for labelling bunk-beds, there are others who will not be—and who would certainly resent any attempt to label them. They might resent feeling the anxiety that would be caused if the labels were used. They might see the label as some sort of intrusion—feeling their own responsibility for their own lives was being questioned or under attack.

The third point, which follows from these two, is that consumers may see labelling not only for the inherent value of the information given, but also as an attempt by someone else to say what they *ought* to do. The fact that the 'someone' may be government may be one possible reason for labelling failing to work as intended. (The consumer may reject information partly by way of 'referred' complaint about other things that governments do.) And the fact that governments, more than producers, will tend to take a normative approach to labelling requirements is another.

In the checklist at the end of this chapter, there are examples of specific kinds of information that may be of use. In the meantime, bear in mind that the value of information—judged in terms of the actual and probable behaviour of consumers in using it—depends on how that information is perceived. This depends on:

Relevance—that. is, providing qualitative or quantitative advantage to consumers, such as a guarantee of a superior quality or standard.

Acceptability—that is, objectivity of information; authority and credibility of source; extent to which recommended action relates to consumer norm.

Comprehensibility—that is, the form and context of the information; the interpretation that may be put on it; the extent to which the instruction, and the reasons for it, are understood.

Conspicuousness—that is, the position, prominence and permanence of the label; its familiarity or newness; and its accessibility to consumers at the time and in the place the information may be needed.

Costs

If there is one thing that symbolises what packaging is, and what labelling could be, it is the recommendation by some consumer groups that the labels on certain products should include information about the cost of the pack.

The extent and cost of waste in packaging is astonishing. In 1974 it was estimated that packaging added up to 8p per lb. weight to the cost of fruit and vegetables sold in supermarkets;[5] and that the average London household threw out over 30 lbs of useless packaging materials each week.[6] In the same year, a reporter from *The Sunday Times* compared two (highly selective) shopping lists of goods—one packed the other not—and found that the prepacked items cost £3.49½, compared with £2.40½ for the others. Items on the list included curtain rings (20p packed, 6p unpacked) and a sink plug (11p packed, 7p loose).[7]

The significance of the cost of packaging may be judged from the following (1975–early 1976) data from the study by the Price Commission into 'The Unit Prices of Small Packs':[8]

Product*	Direct costs per unit of volume/weight of:		
	Ingredients %	Packaging %	Labour %
Processed peas	31	60	9
Canned soup	68	31	1
Baked beans	66	32	2
Instant coffee	79	17	4
Brown sauce	28	42	30
Garden peas	43	38	19
Liquid antiseptic	6	83	11
Washing-up liquid	65	25	10
Gloss paint	72	16	12
Emulsion paint	68	17	15
Fish fingers	85	9	6
Breakfast cereal	48	38	14
Washing powder	76	17	7

* Figures for most popular pack size only.
Reprinted by permission of the Controller of Her Majesty's Stationery Office.

These and more detailed data (for example, on the breakdown of energy, resource and other packaging costs[9]) may say something about the cost of packaging, and also about the cost of designing or formulating products in different ways. For example, the disproportionately high cost of packaging in a high volume/low cost item such as liquid antiseptic should prompt one to ask whether the product could not be totally reformulated—for example, as a tablet or as a concentrate packed in a sachet—and if so, at what other cost.

If savings cannot be made by modifying the product, what can be done about the cost of the packaging itself? Briefly, there are four things:

Design of packaging. Consider, for example, possibilities for the use of alternative forms and materials for packaging; or for the use of returnable, reusable or recyclable containers. Avoid overpackaging, particularly of the 'container-within-container' variety, and packaging frills. (There is interesting and plentiful evidence of overpackaging in a 1976 report on packaging by the National Federation of Consumer Groups).

Sizes of products and packages. It nearly always costs relatively more to package a product in small sizes. (In its study of the variations in retail unit price between the smallest, most popular and largest sizes of 16 products—including the 13 listed on the previous page—the Price Commission reported 'unit selling price ratios' of up to 179:100). In some cases, packaging of small quantities—say of cup hooks or wood screws—is absurd. In other cases, the situation is more complicated. For example, many consumers (often including the old and disadvantaged) need to have smaller packs, particularly when buying perishable food. At the same time, the manufacturer is likely to face disproportionately higher production and packaging costs in meeting this need. There may therefore be very little room for manoeuvre—other than by redesigning the packaging of smaller sizes or by offloading some of the cost of producing in smaller sizes elsewhere.

Providing more, relevant information. In particular, further information might be given about (i) the relative unit prices of various sizes; and (ii) the preservation, storage and estimated life of the contents of perishable foods and other goods.

Standardisation of containers. The case for greater standardisation is resisted mainly on the grounds that it makes it difficult for producers to distinguish their brands. The argument is less than compelling, if you consider what different labels do for identical jars or cans. The case for standardisation depends on the possibility of economies in production and storage and, above all, on greater opportunities for the recovery and reuse of containers. One-pint milk bottles are an obvious case in point.

These solutions can be (and frequently are) rejected by producers, on the grounds that, if adopted, they would lead to a decline in sales—so consumers would lose the benefit of economies of scale. The argument is valid only if one is concerned (as individual producers are) about the *direct* costs to consumers of certain individual brands. It is unacceptable—just as it would be if offered as a justification for, say, deceptive packaging—because of the potential savings to be made and shared overall.

In particular, indirect savings could be made on resource and energy use, and on the cost of litter and refuse collection and disposal—but these are not problems with which individual producers (or indeed consumers) are generally required to be concerned. There is evidence of their lack of concern, for example in the use of packaging materials such as board made irrecoverable simply because of the inscriptions in plastic print, or the use of wet-strength additives which prevent repulping. (And what consumer magazine ever recommended against the use of a product on grounds such as these?)

In short, while the producer answers for his activities only to those who buy his products (and they are intermediate users rather than the consumers of packaging) he might also be called to account for costs imposed on society at large. First, he might answer for the use of resources of real value, to produce packaging which may have virtually none. Secondly, he might answer for imposing costs on those compelled to consume his packaging waste. And finally, he might be answerable for the use of resources which may never be recovered for some better use at another time or place.

Checklist on Packaging and Labelling

The following questions are intended both to summarise and amplify the main issues raised in the preceding chapter. They should be used in conjunction with the general questions relating to policy, organisation, procedures, resources and effects listed in Chapter 3 (pages 27 to 36); and also with the list of standards identified in Chapter 2 (pages 17 to 25).

Physical containment
(1) Is the package appropriately designed, having regard to its function in:

—preventing physical damage or contamination of, or by, the product?
—preserving or storing the product before or during use?

—ensuring the security of the product before or during use?
—identifying the measure of the product, and its quality?
—dispensing the product, allowing repeated and/or measured use?

Comments

Evidence on the adequacy of packaging (in providing protection for the product) may be found by examining records of complaints and the action taken on them; and by looking for evidence of accidental use or misuse, particularly by children and especially where medicines and bottled household and garden products are concerned.

There are numerous legal requirements relating to both packaging and labelling, particularly where food and dangerous substances are concerned. (For background information please refer to list of standards in Chapter 2, pages 17 to 25. Otherwise, refer to more specialised publications, some of which are listed in the Appendix to this book.)

British Standards Institution has published several standards, mainly concerned with the strength of packaging materials. These are briefly described in Sectional List No. 15, available free from BSI.

The Institute of Packaging does not publish a code of practice for members (nor do they make publicly available a list of member individuals). The Institute runs courses and seminars on various aspects of packaging, which are open to members only.

The Packaging Industry Research Association publishes information on the cost and availability of raw packaging materials in its 'Statistical and Economic Review of Packaging'. They also publish occasional research reports (details on request from their Leatherhead office, telephone number: 03723 76161).

Attention should be paid to packaging which could mislead about the quality or quantity of contents. For instance, the 1975–76 annual report of the Cleveland County Consumer Protection Office refers to the likelihood of 4-litre paint cans being mistaken for 5-litre ones. Similarly, at present, 12 oz jars of jam are easily mistaken for 1 lb ones; and the difference between the familiar and traditional size of a bottle of spirits, and the slightly smaller sizes which have started to appear, is detectable only by meticulous scrutiny of the label. In the absence of unit pricing, the use of non-standard pack sizes (that is, $6\frac{3}{4}$ oz or 321 cc) can only confuse or mislead.

Deceptions may also occur when a package profile clearly suggests there is more of the product than there in fact is. *Which?* (January 1976, p. 12) shows a classic example of this with Astral Skin Cream. Another is Procter and Gamble's Head and Shoulders shampoo: the ingredients are contained in a bottle, tapered in all dimensions, and the bottle is contained, for no good apparent reason, in an oblong cardboard pack. The volume of the ingredients is equal to about 45 per cent of the volume of the pack.

Equally, a pack or container may mislead about the quality of a product. A good example is Libby's Orange 'C'—which is an orange drink, not a juice, but which is sold in jars similar to the kind orange juice is frequently sold in. (By law, an 'orange drink' has to contain only 10 per cent of orange juice.)

Bear in mind also that the design of any packaging which allows the measured use of a product will influence the rate at which a product is used. For example, with a 200 cc tube of toothpaste, you would get about 160 1 cm squeezes from a nozzle with a 4 mm diameter. But if the diameter of the nozzle were (almost imperceptibly) increased to 5 mm, you would get only about 100 1 cm squeezes.

Labelling and information

(2) Should, and does, the labelling on the product clearly give information about any or all of the following:

—Product origin, including name and address of manufacturer and/or holding company and/or agent or distributor; batch, stock or model number or description; trade mark; country of origin and date of manufacture?

—General description of contents, including information about size, weight, capacity, rating, etc., and reference to applications and limitations in use?

—Specific description of contents, including information such as list of ingredients by proportion; unit price; energy efficiency or consumption; characteristic properties of ingredients—such as the nutritional value; and an indication of the main or active ingredients and the percentage thereof?

—The quality or performance rating—including the mark of the grade or class or produce and any certification or approval mark indicating compliance with a standard?

—Any special terms of sale, including the recommended price, any special offer or discount, and any exclusions or attempted exclusions from liability?

—Relevant instructions and information relating to the storage, transportation, assembly, use, repair or replacement of parts; or the cleaning, maintenance or servicing; or disposal of the product?

—Any special instructions, warnings or information relating to any of the above; or relating to emergency procedures and antidotes; or to use by special classes of consumers—such as children, or people suffering from certain illnesses or allergies, or on special diets?

Comments

The relative importance of packaging as a means of physical containment and as a source of information is indicated by the type and numbers of complaints received by the Office of Fair Trading. In an average year (extrapolating from figures for the first quarter of 1976) the OFT gets around 1000 complaints about packaging and about 15 000 complaints of lack of information—much of which could have been given on the pack:

Type of complaint	Annual number of complaints
Packaging which may mislead as to size or quality of contents	420
Packaging which is overelaborate	190
Packaging which creates disposal problems	60
Other	380
Complaints relating to lack of information about:	
Performance specification or use	880
Care and maintenance	780
Selling price	300
Terms and conditions of sale	2180
Age of perishable goods and date by which they should be sold	80
How to register a complaint	930
Origin of goods	300
Other	3590

In each of the areas listed in the questions above, an assessment should be made of (a) the relevance and completeness of information, (b) the acceptability of the information given, (c) comprehensibility, and (d) its conspicuousness.

A fair example of irrelevant information is the slogan: 'Guaranteed anthrax free' found on an unbranded shaving brush in a market in the late 1960s. By contrast, the statement of percentage of active ingredient on the pack of Sainsbury's washing-up liquid would be entirely relevant if other manufacturers gave comparable information (which they usually do not).

One useful way of checking the relevance of information on a product label is to compare what is on the label with the information given in the product's design or performance specification. For instance, if the design or formulation of the product includes a preservative of any kind, there is a clear case for stating on the pack how the product should stored and how long it will last.

Similarly, to check the completeness of any information given, compare what consumers are told with what the manufacturer has established that they need. For example, car manufacturers know that consumers may overload their cars—so could not cars be labelled or marked with a 'Plimsoll line' (in the form of a sliding scale between the wheel and wheel-arch) to indicate the degree of load?

To judge the acceptability of information—apart from totally spurious messages such as 'new' or 'improved'—you need to know how consumers are likely to respond to a message they understand, and why they do or do not respond in certain ways. For example, most people will not 'fasten seat belts' if those belts are designed like spaghetti and are hard to fasten. Similarly, many people do not respond to the warning that gas boards slapped on the side of older and potentially dangerous open-flued gas water heaters—'do not run water while you are in the bath'—perhaps mainly because the instruction is unreasonably demanding. If you are lying in a cooling bath, it is natural to heat it up by running in more hot water. The instruction not to do so—the significance of which went unexplained —seemed to have been handed down from a bureaucrat with central heating to others without it. (Incidentally, two deaths with such heaters, in 1975, involved men who normally bathed for over an hour each day, in accordance with religious custom, and who were not native English speakers. This may shed further light on the question of 'acceptability' : labels must be acceptable to *all* concerned.)

With comprehensibility, you might check three main things. First, there is the question of what different consumers can and cannot understand. The question of 'functional competence' is touched on towards the end of Chapter 8—but to give an example, there are an estimated 2 million adults in the UK with a reading ability which is below the norm for a nine-year-old. The implications of this are obvious.

Secondly, it is important to know how familiar consumers may be with information contained in marks and symbols. For example, 'care labelling' symbols are widely used on clothing, yet many consumers have no real idea what they mean. (See Linda Christmas on the ineffectiveness of such schemes, in *The Guardian*, 1 September 1976.)

Finally, there is a fair amount of information given in code—which consumers are positively discouraged from understanding. Check what coded information means, whether it would be of any use if explained, and whether the manufacturer will explain its meaning on request. The use of codes may be justified—when the information is boring, or to save space—but it often is not.

The conspicuousness of all this information may be crucial. See, for example, an account of the deaths by chlorine poisoning of two elderly women who mixed chlorine bleach with an ammonia powder cleaner, in defiance or ignorance of an inconspicuous label on the bottle of bleach (*Consumer Reports*, February 1976, p. 66). No information on the label should be given undue prominence. Conversely, any important information should be plain to see.

Cost, conservation and protection of the environment

(3) Has packaging been designed to keep cost as low as it reasonably might be ?

(4) Has the pack been designed in such a way as to minimise waste, the use of energy, and scarce resources ?

(5) Does the packaging allow, as appropriate, for reuse in the original or new application ; recycling, including ease of segregation ; and/or safe and economical compaction, degradation or disposal ?

Comments

An evaluation should be made of the cost of the packaging and of the savings to be made by consumers and by society at large, by redesign. Information about conservation and environmental issues should be sought from specialist sources, including Friends of the Earth, Waste Management Advisory Council, local authorities, and other bodies mentioned earlier in the text.

7 Marketing and Competition

Marketing may include anything to do with demand for a company's products. At the very least, it entails selling to people who present themselves to buy. At most, it may have a profound influence not only on consumer demand, but also on what is made and how it is distributed and sold.

In an extreme case, marketing may be everything and the product nothing—at least, nothing more than a symbolic reminder of the image offered for sale. 'Pet Rocks'—in other words, ordinary stones, packaged and sold as 'pets' and guaranteed to be obedient, loyal, housetrained and otherwise undemanding, etc.—are the ultimate expression of this. What distinguished pet rocks from billions of other rocks was the image imparted by the marketing. The rocks sold presumably because they acquired some magic value, despite the tongue-in-cheek marketing approach. The magic could be compared to that of something revered as the relic of a saint—despite its unerring resemblance to any old bone.

By contrast, the product could be everything, and the marketing virtually nothing. Mousetraps may be one of the last few such products around—and, as such, will be used as a worked (and totally imaginary) example, to outline the influence marketing may have in every major business function. See Table 5 below.

Standards

It should be acknowledged that this is only one point of view in an area where there is room for many more—not least because this underlines the lack of any clear, comprehensive and generally accepted guidelines about what marketing methods are acceptable, and what are not. The inadequacy of the standards there are—an inadequacy which seems painful in the light of the fact that it is, by present-day standards, perfectly normal and acceptable to commit human and other resources to duping the public into buying vermin control

Table 5

Issue or imperative	Possible strategy for marketing mousetraps	Comment
Sales, etc. overview. State of the market and general prospects for sales. Sales and market trends. Competitors' activities and brand shares. Past, present and projected volume and value of sales, etc.	Two problems: (i) the market is wide open to anyone who can saw wood and bend wire, and is also small—and this rules out possibility of controlling market by taking over the competition.; (ii) the poison-bait people have large and growing share of market, and dominate supply to rodent control firms. Possible solutions: acquire interest in these firms and diversify into bait—or re-establish need for traps by breeding bait-resistant strains of mice and 'freeing' them	If you think either of these proposed solutions is implausible, read Barry Commoner on General Motors, in *The Poverty of Power*[1]. When, in the 1930s, GM's salesmen found it hard to sell their new line of petrol-engined buses, the company's solution was to systematically take over and close down all the electric tram and bus companies they could. It worked. (GM was later fined a piddling $5000 for criminal conspiracy, and its treasurer—who had helped to break up Los Angeles's $100 m streetcar system—was fined one dollar)

The product, etc. What it is, how it is made, what materials are used, how it compares with competitors' products, what technical possibilities exist for improving it, what chance there is that the product might be made totally obsolescent— for example if an effective gas or electronic mouse exterminator were introduced

Product is unexciting and lacks brand distinctiveness. Sales are slow, because it can be, and is, used again and again. Solution is to add a product feature. New trap will incorporate black plastic 'shroud' attached to wire snapper—capable of being folded or extended in the manner of a pram hood. This will give consumer satisfaction (because mouse is simultaneously killed and buried, and need not be extricated from trap) and will also ensure that trap is thrown away with mouse (thus creating demand for new trap)

In principle, there is nothing implausible about this either. Indeed, there are countless examples of 'improvements' of this kind in almost every type of product. But have we really nothing better to do, that we allow massive resources to be devoted to, say, improving the viscosity of tomato sauce?

Pricing, profits and costs, etc. Establish main cost elements—that is manufacture and distribution. Determine what people would be prepared to pay (upper threshold) for different designs of trap. Check likely trends for future costs (for example, cost of black plastic sheet). Relate pricing policy to company objectives (for example, quick profit or slower growth)

Patented design of trap minimises possibility of imitation—and 'up-market' design and promotional strategy call for premium price—but one which must be compatible with expected demand for product, and ultimately acceptable to retailer and consumer alike

The purpose of a patent is ultimately to encourage innovation, by rewarding it. On the other hand, patents may be, and are, used to extract extortionate rewards—or, failing this, to block the introduction of a badly needed product. Note that consumers may pay more (a) if product *appears* expensive; and (b) if there are fewer points of comparison between it and other products

Issue or imperative	Possible strategy for marketing mousetraps	Comment
Distribution, etc. Where—by region and type of outlet—should product be sold, and what sales force should be used to distribute it? How should product be packaged, displayed and sold: for example, should traps be sold in pairs, in multipacks or as single units? What promotions/incentives might be offered to dealer to advance sales, apart from evidence of forthcoming consumer advertising programme? How much time, space or inconvenience would there be in promotions involving: (a) distribution of free samples to consumers, (b) coupons or money-off offers, (c) a competition open either to dealers or consumers, (d) cash or quantity discount for dealer, (e) gift or bribe to dealer or staff, (f) in-store demonstration of product, (g) use of reusable and returnable containers, (h) on-pack special offer, or offer of discount to consumer on next purchase	Research establishes that retailer resistance to mousetraps—due to the probable embarrassment of consumers who buy them—prevents display. 'We stock them, but don't sell them—except in paper bags,' was one typical dealer response. Possible solutions: overcome consumer resistance, and/or completely switch to other outlets. Obvious possibilities are chemists, because they are trusted for their discretion by consumers, and would also lend 'class' to the product, and emphasise the importance of health and hygiene in mouse control. Alternative: stick with the problem of consumer resistance and embarrassment, and try mail-order or go door-to-door	The importance of the retailer's role in selling products—and the reasons why retailers display or actively sell some brands more than others—have traditionally been underestimated by 'consumer watchdogs'. The degree of control (sometimes through ownership) over retail outlets, in particular by major brand producers, can effectively stop competition from others. At the same time, competition between producers for the time, space and co-operation of retailers' ranges from the intense to cut-throat. This area deserves closer examination than it usually gets

Consumer strategy, etc. Establish target consumers and what characteristics the product must be seen (or not seen) by them to have. Check patterns of purchasing and use; and place, time and method of use. Establish psychological and other factors which may influence resistance to product, or acceptance of it. Determine how to reach these consumers (media and message) and plan promotional and advertising campaign accordingly

Points to emphasise to consumers: 'health risks', a 'hidden problem', 'a universal and growing problem' (so do not be complacent or ashamed). Points to de-emphasise: (a) do not say *mice* (living and even lovable creatures) say *vermin;* (b) do not *kill* them, merely *control them.* Means of emphasis: get a public relations firm to 'inspire' a few press or TV features on the vermin problem. Make TV commercials using 'Anne, Duchess of Neasden', or whoever, to show how she controls the problem in her mansion or stately home. If *she* can, anyone can. Use back-up advertisements— stressing 'from all good chemists'— in press.

Such deviousness is entirely commonplace—as numerous examples show. It arises particularly in highly competitive markets, where real (technological) product differentiation is slight—as is more and more often the case. It is fostered within organisations where executives can become unashamed to make remarks like this—even in jest—about their own competitive spirit: "I'll cheat my kids at cards if that's what it takes to win. Somebody once said, "winning is not the most important thing . . . it's the *only* thing!" I agree'. (A general manager in major US car firm, quoted in *Consumer Reports.*[2]

modules and similar rubbish—is characterised by three main things. These are:

—that acceptable behaviour is defined by exception—and tends also to be judged by the means employed, rather than by the effects of employing them;

—that this is an area in which self-regulation (and therefore the influence of the industry) is strong. This is explained by the fact that governments tend to be unwilling to commit the considerable resources it would take to control marketing activity effectively; and partly because of the political sensitivity of the issue. Where the control of advertising is concerned, governments would be open to (at least the advertisers') cries of 'Censorship';

—that there is a strong tradition of weak enforcement, partly because of this—and also because this is an area in which enforcement is extremely difficult. This is both because of the many nuances of deception, and also because deception is not often evident on the face of things.

The main laws relating to the methods used in marketing and advertising are listed in Chapter 2 (pages 17 to 19). (Other, less important statutes are listed in the Appendix of the 'British Code of Advertising Practice' published by the Advertising Standards Authority Ltd.)

There are many voluntary codes and standards which relate to marketing. Again, these are concerned mainly with marketing methods and means, rather than effects and ends. They also characteristically overlap and are not universally binding: they apply only to the individuals or organisations affiliated to the body which issues the standard. The main codes and standards include:[3]

British Institute of Management—Code of Best Practice, 1974
Code of Advertising Practice (CAP) Committee—British Code of Advertising Practice and British Code of Sales Promotion Practice (both 1974)
Institute of Marketing—Code of Practice, 1973
Institute of Public Relations—Code of Conduct, 1975
International Chamber of Commerce—Codes of Marketing Practice: (a) Advertising; (b) Marketing Research; and (c) Sales Promotion, all 1974; and Guidelines for the application of the Code of Sales Promotion Practice, 1975
Market Research Society and Industrial Market Research Association —Code of Conduct, 1973
Sales Promotion Executives Association—Code of Practice, 1971

There is one exception to the general rule—that these codes and laws are concerned mainly with the means of marketing, rather than the ends—and this is the principle of fair trading. Fair trading is legally implied to *exclude* any:

commercial activities . . . which relate to goods supplied to consumers . . . or which relate to services supplied . . . which may adversely affect the interests (whether they are economic interests or interests with respect to health, safety or other matters) of consumers in the United Kingdom.[4]

However, the usefulness of this definition· is as a guideline for disclosure and reporting by auditors—rather than as a standard against which marketing or other practices could be judged to be on one side or another of the law. The extract quoted is not a description of what is malpractice and what is not. It relates only to the (discretionary) duties of the Director General of Fair Trading to 'keep under review' and to 'receive and collate evidence' of what appears to be malpractice. Furthermore, a clear distinction is made between practice which affects the 'economic interests' and other interests of consumers— the Director General being concerned far more about economic issues than anything else.

In short, standards for marketing are comparable to those for production, in emphasising means rather than ends. The standards that affect design and manufacture relate to the ways in which a producer achieves his intended goal, rather than to the value of the goals themselves. In the same way, marketing can be directed at highly questionable ends (mousetraps and beyond) provided it does not use totally unacceptable means to do so.

Double standards

Certainly the means used in production or marketing are important— but the ends are probably even more so. You can see their relative significance if you consider how criticism of the methods used in some TV commercial and other advertisements could be—but actually are not—applied equally to public service announcements and the like. For example, you could—but probably would not—criticise a familiar announcement urging people to use seat belts on any one of the following grounds:

Point of criticism	Illustration of relevance
Uses testimonial from celebrity, and emphasises experience of untypical users	Jimmy Savile, the presenter of the 'clunk-click' ads brings on particularly tragically damaged victims
Uses statistics in a way which could mislead	Some ads emphasise that most accidents occur close to home—but do not say either how much driving is done close to home, or whether these are the most significant *injury-producing* accidents
Advertisements appeal to fear of viewer	Yes, they do
Advertisements do not give information you may need	For example, they do not tell you whether you will *always* be safer in a seat belt
The advertisements stress unusual situations	Yes, they stress the agony of going through the windscreen, rather than the everyday inconvenience, for some, of wrestling with spaghetti-like belts

These and several other criticisms which could be made of a lowly seat-belt announcement would apply even more to many other sweeping and unsubstantiated claims, accepted as part of everyday life (for example, those which underlie virtually any organised religion).

But that is not the point. The point is that the so-called *natural virtues* (prudence, temperance, fortitude and justice—as advertised on TV in public service spots) and the theological virtues (faith, hope and love—at least in the unbranded version) are, in principle, unquestionably worth believing in.

This point has not been lost on advertisers who dress up their appeals in acknowledgements of the consumer's natural virtue— virtue which of course should have its own brand of reward:

Virtue	Reward, etc.
Prudence	You're *wise* to do this, and you're *right* to do that. You *know* it makes sense, etc., etc.
Temperance	Go on: spoil yourself . . . (in other words as a reward for being so temperate up to now)
Fortitude	You've had a hard day: Now relax with . . . (Again, the advertiser suggests a modest reward for acknowledged fortitude on the part of the consumer)
Justice	Would you deny your children . . . ? Or even: You owe it to yourself . . . (or justice begins at home and, whatever it is, it is fairly due)

Provided neither the alleged nor actual value of the product (nor the motive of the producer) is seriously in question, then the appeal may be persuasive. Those at whom such appeals are directed will probably go along as—at least willing and perhaps, knowing— partners in any little deceptions involved.

Causes and effects

In other cases, the means used in marketing may be less acceptable— for their effects either on people as consumers, or on society at large. Marketing can directly harm consumers, and indirectly cause more general harm, by:

—compounding the harm of products by promoting their use (cigarettes, for example);

—contributing negatively to the design of products (cars, for example);

—overemphasising the virtues of a product, and misleading consumers in doing so—sometimes in cases in which the product would otherwise be entirely acceptable (for example, certain promotions for the use of powdered milk baby foods in the third world).

The most visible harm is done by advertising. Specifically, advertising has been criticised for: pandering and otherwise debasing tastes and values; and for portraying fantasised, overidealised or stereotyped images of people, which may be offensive and alienating to substantial numbers of people who do not belong to (or at least identify with) the 'target group'.

If it is not always possible to judge or measure such effects, it should be possible at least to show how they arise. 'Failures' may happen by accident or design—or by something in between:

Accident—that is, where the possibility of a harmful effect has been entirely (and perhaps understandably) overlooked, and where no such effect was intended.

Ill-judgement—that is, where the possibility of harmful effect might have been appreciated but was not, or where the extent of harm was underestimated—and where failure of either kind was not intended to have occurred.

Default—that is, where a harmful effect is anticipated but is nevertheless neither intended nor wanted as such.

Design—that is, where the effect was anticipated and calculated.

When failure or malpractice is acknowledged by a producer and corrected—particularly without prompting or intervention from outside—this is one thing. But what about cases in which there is repeated and unchecked failure against what the Retail Trading Standards Association calls 'The Acid Test': 'An announcement or practice is inaccurate or misleading if, intentionally or otherwise, it may lead shoppers to believe that merchandise in general, or any specific article, is more desirable than is actually the case'?[5]

One positive thing that may be done is to use objective methods (for example, copy-testing, to assess what advertisements are *taken* to mean) either to justify or question the frequently made assumption that no accepted marketing practice prevents consumers from distinguishing between reality and appearance. But this still leaves a vast area of practically untestable marketing practices—whose effect, in relation to the products involved, bears a striking resemblance to the aforementioned itching 'Lotion A' and its relief-giving counterpart, 'Lotion B' (see page 9).

Ultimately one can question only the motives of those who create the illusions, rather than the illusions of those who suffer them.

Checklist on Marketing and Competition

The following questions are intended both to summarise and amplify the main issues raised in the preceding chapter. They should be used in conjunction with the general questions relating to policy, organisation, procedures, resources and effects listed in Chapter 3 (pages 27 to 36); and also with the list of standards identified in Chapter 2 (pages 17 to 25).

Market position

(1) Does the company dominate in any market and thereby take improper advantage of its position? Or does it operate (or can it be expected to operate) in a manner conducive to the 'public interest', in other words by:

—producing by the most efficient and economical means, and at such volumes and prices as will best meet home and overseas market requirements?

—being organised in such a way as to encourage greater efficiency and new enterprise?

—making the best and fullest use of men, materials and industrial capacity?

—and by the full development of technical improvements, the expansion of existing markets, and by the development of new markets?

Comments

Article 86 of the Treaty of Rome forbids any company to take improper advantage of a dominant market position. (In the UK, a dominant position is taken to mean at least a one-quarter share of a market.)

In determining whether a company does or may operate in the public interest, the UK Monopolies Commission would consider such factors as are listed above, as well as other aspects of the company's structure, organisation and performance. In past judgements, the importance attached to different factors has varied—and there are no hard and fast rules about what is acceptable and what is not.

Legislation on monopolies, restrictive practices and other practices which may 'adversely affect' the economic interests of consumers is enforced by the Office of Fair Trading (OFT). There are no significant voluntary standards relating thereto.

Criteria used by the Office of Fair Trading for assessing the impact of monopoly and related power have been described in the paper, 'The Development of an Economic Information System for Selecting Monopoly References'. This paper (available from OFT) refers to certain 'conduct' and 'performance' indicators by which companies' behaviour may be judged. The following would be particularly relevant in a social audit:

Conduct indicators

(i) Numbers of trade and consumer complaints made to the OFT (and confidential to the OFT).

(ii) Evidence or allegations about price leadership or price parallelism obtained from various sources (see *Parallel Pricing*, Cmnd. 5330, (London HMSO, 1973)).

(iii) The advertising/sales ratio of those industries using advertising.

(iv) The acquisitions indicator.

Performance indicators

(i) Return on capital (expressed both as change in margins, and change in capital turnover).

(ii) Contribution to inflation (the 'inflation relative' being calculated 'by dividing the percentage change in the wholesale price index for the products in question by the percentage change in the relevant index of material and fuel input prices').

For further information, refer to the select bibliography, *Competition, Monopoly and Restrictive Practices* (HMSO, 1970) and to *Mergers* (A Guide to Board of Trade Practice (HMSO, 1969)) ; and to annual reports of the Office of Fair Trading.

Competition policy

(2) Does the company take part in (or is it involved in) any action which may result in the 'prevention, restriction or distortion of competition'—such as price fixing, restrictive practices or information agreements—whether or not the detrimental effects of such practices may be expected to be outweighed by such possible benefits as :

—protecting the public against injury (for example, in the case of an agreement relating to exchange of information about material, process or product hazards) ;

—removing the threat of serious and/or persistent unemployment in the area(s) in which the trade is located ;

—increasing the volume or earnings of export business ;

—providing the public with specific and substantial benefits, and/or avoiding such specific detrimental effects as : reduction in the quality or variety of quality of products ; increases in the prices of products in the long term ; reduction of points of sale ; or deterioration of after-sales service.

Comments

Article 85 of the Treaty of Rome specifically forbids actions which may result in the 'prevention, restriction or distortion of competition'— and in particular any form of price fixing or cartel.

Judgements under UK restrictive practice legislation generally follow the pattern described above—in that all arrangements and agreements are presumed to operate *against* the public interest unless exceptional circumstances prevail. Examples of such exceptional circumstances are given above.

In UK law, it is not necessarily illegal to be party to an arrangement or agreement, but it is illegal not to register the agreement, or to be party to any agreement already proscribed. The onus is on companies concerned to show why exemptions may or should be given in the case of any particular agreement.

Pricing and profits

(3) Are the company's pricing methods fair, and its target profit levels reasonable, having regard to (a) the market dominance of the company in the supply of particular goods or services; and (b) the dependence of consumers on the company for their supply?

(4) To what extent do the company's pricing policies reflect (a) its actual costs in making and selling the product; and (b) its ability to set and command certain price levels by virtue of its dominance in a market sector?

(5) Has the company failed to enter, or withdrawn from competition in, any area (particularly where consumers do or would depend largely on it) simply because it estimated that return on its investment would be below an acceptable level? If so, what is that level, and could it by any measure be described as 'excessive'?

(6) Has the company used its 'technological knowhow' unreasonably restrictively—for example, as a significant market barrier to competitors—and what has been the effect of such restrictions?

Comments

There are three main techniques used in pricing—or four, if you include 'intuition'. First, there is the 'cost-plus' approach, in which price is set by reference to manufacturing, distribution, promotion and other costs, plus taxes and profit. 'Differential pricing' involves setting prices mainly by reference to the prices set by competitors, or near or would-be competitors. Finally, there is the 'demand analysis' approach: here, estimated consumer demand is related to different possible prices, the price being fixed at the level which offers the best return.

In pricing a product, a manufacturer will certainly be likely to use both the cost-plus and differential-pricing methods to establish (a) what the product can be made for; and (b) whether consumers will pay that amount and more. These two approaches at least imply that supply is responsive to demand, assuming that reasonable profit margins are involved.

However, in demand analysis the situation is partly reversed: an estimate is made of probable demand, given different circumstances of supply—and then the products are actually supplied on the terms most favoured by the supplier. The research reports that are prepared in the course of such analyses (invariably confidential) make very depressing reading. This extract, from a survey of potential readers of illustrated 'partworks', shows the kind of thing that goes on:

> From this survey, it can be seen that 34 per cent agree that 40p is 'not a great deal to pay', and that 30 per cent agree that 45p is 'not a great deal to pay'. So a price level of 45p does not seem likely to limit sales to a lower level than we have predicted.

On the question of profit margins, it should be pointed out (a) that there is no simple or single definition of an excessive profit; and (b) it may be quite as important to examine the level of a company's 'discretionary expenditure' as it is to examine the level of its profits. Profit is not strictly a measure of what is surplus to a company's immediate requirements: it is a measure of what the company *thinks* is surplus to its requirements. There is a good deal of expenditure besides, which is well above what is required to run a business effectively and efficiently, and which is attributed to running costs but not declared as profit.

For this reason, the criteria used in every 'official' determination of what is excessive profit, and what is not, takes into account such things as the efficiency of the company (particularly with respect to attaining quality and quantity production) and reduction of costs and economy in the use of materials, manpower and plant. Many such determinations have been made—for example, by the UK Price Commission, the Public Accounts Committee, the US Renegotiation Board and the US General Accounting Office. In addition to the factors listed above, these bodies also consider factors like the level of normal earnings (for example, in one particular industry or for manufacturing industry as a whole), the amount and source of captial employed, the degree of risk assumed, the character of the business and the complexities of production.

Finally, the matter of restriction of technological knowhow not only raises questions about the cost and availability of a firm's products, and of consumers' need for them—but also raises wider questions about the effects of dependence on particular companies, particularly for developing countries. These issues are of great importance, but beyond the scope of this book.

Marketing strategy and policies

(7) How has the company's marketing strategy affected the quality and value of its products, and the character of innovation?

(8) How has this strategy affected the selling methods used by the company to promote its products?

Comments

The value of product developments can be judged not only by the nature and extent of the benefits given (see Chapter 4) but also by the degree of value in relation to (a) the company's own superseded products; (b) competing products which already exist; and (c) products which *might* exist.

In assessing the character of innovation, take account of (a) the options apparently open to the company; (b) its reasons for taking some options, not others; and (c) what it actually achieves.

What most companies aim for and achieve most of the time is a succession of so-called 'evolutionary products', whose significance at the low end of the scale is negligible, but which increases as they become more 'revolutionary' in design. These terms are Roderick White's. In *Consumer Product Development* (Harmondsworth: Pelican 1976, p. 33) White suggests that products can be ranked on 'a novelty scale which ranges from the spuriously or hardly new to the completely new . . .' His scale is proposed as a measure of newness, but it could be useful in describing the degree of benefit a product might bring, as well (see below).

Evolutionary products	New pack size/new pack
	New flavour/perfume/colour
	Variant on existing company product
	'Me-too' product, new to company
	Improved product, new to company
	Significant improvement on existing company product
	Significant improvement on product new to company
Revolutionary products	New product
	Major technological breakthrough

When assessing the direction of a company's effort and the level of its achievement, particular attention should be paid to what the company does not do or try to do. For example, if you were examining a drug company, you might start by asking yourself about unsolved medical and social problems which drugs might cure—and also about non-drug treatments. You might follow this up with questions like: 'What has the company done to try to develop a smoking cure?' or 'Has the company investigated the problems and possiblities of acupuncture?' Only by asking such questions (and perhaps by risking asking some stupid ones) can you hope to establish what a company is really all about. (In this case, there are at least three possible answers: making money, making pills, and finding cures.)

So, newness as such does not really matter. What matters is significance and—to mimic the scale above—this might be assessed along the following lines.

Negligible or illusory significance	Change of little or no significance either for consumers or for the company's competitors
	Change whose main significance is to allow product to become or remain (more) competitive
	Change which improves company's own product by significantly extending its performance without commensurate increase in cost
	Change which improves on a class or range of products by extending their performance (or solving significant problems associated with them) without commensurate increase in cost
	Product which opens up significant new possibilities, or which solves significant problems (not associated with the use of that class or type of product)
Real and major significance	Product which solves major, universal problems, whether natural or manmade, but not associated with or created by that class or type of product

Turning to the question of marketing strategy and selling methods, account might be taken of the company's:

Priorities—for example, including the short/longer-term maximisation of sales; increasing market share or improving competitive position; improved or increased reputation or goodwill; greater or wider consumer 'awareness' and/or distribution of products.

Methods—for example, including the extent and type of consumer promotions; the methods used to influence retailers' stocking, display and sales policies; the use of advertising as a possible barrier to competition; or improving the availability of products in the appropriate quality or range.

Several relevant performance indicators have already been mentioned—for example, reduction of consumer complaints, or assessments of consumer response to different promotional techniques (see, for instance, the annual reports produced by Harris International Shopping and Promotion Intelligence). But there are other ways in which advertising or promotion may directly or indirectly affect the price, quality or range of products available to consumers.

Two particularly useful sources of information on these are *Sales Promotion Handbook*, edited by Tony Dakin (Epping: Gower Press, 1974) which discusses in general and unconsciously uninhibited terms the many different ways in which marketing people try to get through to, or at, consumers. The other, more serious work discusses (by reference to a number of case histories) the impact of advertising, in relation to other variables such as quality and price, on competitive standing and sales. This is the paper, 'Advertising, Competition and Market Conduct—a Statistical Investigation in Western European Countries', by Professor Jean-Jacques Lambin (Amsterdam; *North Holland Series: Contributions to Economic Analysis*, 1975).

Advertising standards

(9) To what extent may the company's advertising deprive consumers of the freedom *not* to buy either a particular brand or class of product, by:

—its volume, insistence and repetition?

—its emphasis on the human motivation in buying, rather than on the qualities in the product worth selling?

(10) To what extent may the company's advertising misinform or mislead consumers about the qualities or performance of the product?

(11) To what extent may the company's advertising lead to unwelcome or unwanted secondary effects, such as:

—promoting the use of a product among 'non-target' consumers (for example, drinking, smoking promoted among children)?

—promoting undesirable behaviour (for example, children nagging or pressurising parents for advertised or displayed products)?

—proving offensive to, or exploiting, the tastes or susceptibilities of significant numbers of individuals or groups of people (such as older people, black minorities, disabled people)?

Comments

Several statutes relating to advertising standards were referred to in Chapter 2. These mainly relate to misleading advertising; they only touch on the question of taste (question (10) above), and have virtually nothing to do with the issues raised in question (9).

Of the voluntary controls referred to in the preceding chapter, he most significant is the 'British Code of Advertising Practice'. The Code and the enforcement system were revised in 1974–75 (see

Social Audit Nos. 1 and 5) and at the time of writing are said to be under review by the Office of Fair Trading (OFT Annual Report 1976, p. 17).

The 'British Code of Advertising Practice' (BCAP) basically requires that advertisements be 'legal, decent, honest and truthful'—but, so far as honesty and truth are concerned, not wholly so. The Code includes both specific and also general provisions. For example, advertisements 'should be prepared with a sense of responsibility to the consumer' and 'should not be so framed as to abuse the trust of the consumer or exploit his lack of knowledge or understanding'.

Of course, the significance of these requirements depends very largely on the interpretations put on them, and on the vigour and effectiveness of enforcement. The record of the Advertising Standards Authority Ltd—the body under whose general supervision the BCAP is interpreted and enforced—has not persuaded voluntary consumer organisations in the UK of the effectiveness of self-regulation. At the time of writing (mid-1977) most UK consumer interests are actively supporting EEC proposals for the statutory control of advertising.

As has been explained, there are infinite possibilities in advertising for perverting the basis of consumer choice. To test for these, two main methods may be used: (a) objective and independent assessment of the claims made in the light of what is claimed or promised; and (b) the use of copy-testing, to establish the actual impact of advertising on consumers.

Both methods were used in a major and influential study of advertising standards, published by BEUC (*Bureau Européen des Unions des Consommateurs*) in early 1975. In this study, over 3000 advertisements (which had appeared in the national press during a one-month period in the summer of 1974) were examined by research workers with a specialist knowledge of the product or service in question. Of the 3000 advertisements, 430 (14 per cent) were considered misleading, and about half of them were believed to offend both the letter and the spirit of the 'British Code of Advertising Practice'.

Two other aspects of advertising control are worth mentioning briefly. One is corrective advertising—important, partly because any assessment of an advertiser's work should take into account his willingness to correct any misleading impressions given. The second is the substantiation of advertising claims: again, a company's performance might reasonably be judged in the light of its ability and willingness to fully support any claims it makes.

Nevertheless, there is no formal, legal or other requirement at present in the UK which requires advertisers to do either—and there can be little doubt that this encourages abuse. A fair example of this appeared in *Car* magazine (in November 1976). They reported the case of an advertisement which had improbably shown a standard saloon car emerging relatively unscathed from a head-on crash. Only after a rival manufacturer had gone to the expense and trouble of duplicating the test did it become clear that the advertisement actually showed a frame cut from film made in the initial stages of the crash, and well before its full destructive effect had occurred.

Such examples are familiar enough, though many probably go un-detected.

8 After Sales

A producer's after-sales responsibilities to consumers relate to (i) the satisfactory working of products; and (ii) liability for any defects or for any consequential loss. The first of these responsibilities may involve specific commitments in any one or all of the following areas.

Arranging for the product to be delivered or sold in good condition or in proper working order

There is evidence of widespread failure in quality control or pre-delivery inspection—that is, of batch or sample failures as distinct from design faults. Such failures may be more frequent in some products than in others, and may be more or less significant in their effects. For example:

—New cars invariably have defects; while spin driers or vacuum cleaners usually do not. Similarly, some processed foods tend to get contaminated, while others do not (hamburgers and frankfurters, for instance, are notorious for high bacteria counts—and for containing extraneous matter such as insect parts or rodent hairs).

—The defects involved may be essentially insignificant (some 'flash' on a moulded plastic drainpipe, for example); or they may slightly affect the appearance or value of a product, but not the way it works (such as a small scratch or dent in the side of a cooker). More serious are defects which lead to non-function, or to malfunction which may be dangerous (for instance, a missing electrical connection may make a product 'dead', while a wrong connection may make it lethally 'live').

From the consumer's point of view, the significance of a defect of any one kind varies also with the type (and obviously the value) of the product. A defective matchstick or paperclip is one thing; a

100

leaking washing machine or stationary car is another. Defects in all of these products occur—but the more expensive the product, the less acceptable the defect tends to be.

Delivery defects (detected) in major consumer durables appear relatively very high. A 1976 survey of after-sales service in the European Economic Community showed, for example, that in four EEC countries an average 16 per cent of products were found defective on delivery.[1] Similarly, a 1977 *Which?* survey[2] reported defects of the following kinds.

Product	Proportion with defects of any kind	Proportion of defective new products which did not work properly or at all
Dishwashers	one in four	'a quarter did not work properly and a third had functional parts missing or faulty'
Automatic washing machines	one in five	one-third
Twin-tub washing machines	one in six	one-third
Spin driers	very small	negligible
Tumbler driers	one in twelve	not stated
Freezers and refrigerators	one in seven	one in four
Cookers (electric)	one in four	one in five
(gas)	one in three	one in five

Such failures may be attributable to (a) poor quality control, (b) inadequate protection in packaging (for example, one-third of all defective cookers in the *Which?* survey were scratched); and (c) inadequate arrangements made for the prevention and/or cure of defects by dealers and retailers. Alisdair Aird (1972) has commented on the arrangements between UK car manufacturers and dealers, as follows:

Of course, many of the faults in a new car are covered by its guarantee. But, although manufacturers pay garages about £35 million a year for guarantee work, this is 'at prices generally designed to cover costs but which preclude any element of profit'. In this way, manufacturers gain by being paid for work which may not be done until months later, thus increasing their cash flow; by having the work done at lower wage rates than they would have to pay themselves—manual workers in the garage trade are generally paid nearly 20 per cent less than manual workers on the manufacturing side of the industry . . .[3]

The arrangements made by manufacturers for the assembly or installation of their products may be equally important—and may also be comparably bad. For instance, it has been estimated that up to 80 per cent of plumbed-in washing machines and dishwashers could be in breach of official regulations or codes of practice.[4] Similarly, the hazards arising from the faulty installation of gas water heaters—particularly in bathrooms—are recognised in the gas industry, if not widely appreciated elsewhere.

Arrangements made for maintenance, service or repair

Many consumer products—but notably cars and gas heating equipment—should be regularly serviced. And, at one time or another, all products break down and need repair.

The frequency of service needed, and of breakdowns, varies with the age and type of product and, of course, depends on the use it gets. For the products listed in the table on the preceding page, representative figures would be: a one-in-five breakdown rate in the guarantee period (usually the first year of use) and a rate of 50 per cent or more for washing and dishwashing machines and gas cookers, during the first two-and-a-half years of life.

The cost of repairs accounts for a significant part of the 'total life-cycle cost' of many products. In relation to overhead and power costs, the cost of servicing may recently have decreased—but only because of a disproportionate rise in the cost of power since the energy crisis in 1972. Typical (US) servicing costs, before that date, ranged from 6 per cent (refrigerators) to 35 per cent (colour TVs) of the total costs involved.[5] The cost of *not* being able to get equipment repaired would increase this proportion still more.

Consumers will therefore want to know not only how well a product performs, but also what happens when it does not. Specifically, consumers may be concerned about:

—their dependence on third parties (financial and otherwise) for repair and service work;

—whether products have or have not been designed to facilitate fault-diagnosis, repair and service;

—what arrangements have been made for the appointment, training and remuneration of service personnel;

—how (if at all) the work of manufacturers' agents is monitored, to ensure that servicing and repairs are promptly and effectively done, and at a reasonable cost; and

—what arrangements may be made (such as arbitration) for the resolution of problems and disputes between the consumer and the producer or his agents.

Consumers will also be affected by the arrangements made by manufacturers for the following.

The provision of spare parts

In particular, consumers will be affected by the design, the availability and the price of spare parts.

Good design is characterised by (i) the use of standard parts; and (ii) the use of the simplest possible assemblies of parts compatible with performance and with the ease and cost of replacement. The benefits of such policies may include:

—reducing the likelihood of abuse by monopoly suppliers and conversely:

—increasing the likelihood of competition—and thereby increasing the number of sources of spares, and reducing the cost of the spares themselves;

—reducing the stocking burden for the producer and his agents— and also increasing the pool of available spares;

—reducing the waste of resources—for example, by not directing research, development and production capability towards spurious ends; and by avoiding wastage of materials by replacing, so far as possible, only those parts which are spent.

The main justification for the use of non-standardised parts—that is, for changing a design from a standardised to non-standardised form— must be to achieve a very substantial improvement in performance. Such improvement might result either from the discovery of new technology or new materials—or from the realisation of serious inadequacies in an existing design. These inadequacies might become apparent (i) when new data about the part's or product's performance, in normal, abnormal or abuse conditions, became available (from service returns, for example); or (ii) when the performance of an existing standardised part in a new overall design could not be relied upon (for example, because of lack of data about the performance of

the part under new conditions, or because of a known limitation—
such as an inadequate margin of strength.)

Equally, there may be some justification for the use of relatively
complex assemblies such as replacement parts (or for the absence of
spares) when the cost of replacing only a spent part would clearly
be higher than some alternative form of replacement or repair.
For example: if the element in a light bulb burns out, it is obviously
cheaper to buy a complete new assembly of parts (in other words,
a new bulb) than it is to attempt any repair.

In other words, the design of a spare should take into account the
cost of making a part, and also the complexity and cost involved in
fitting it. At the same time, the increasing trend to the supply of sealed
assemblies of parts—particularly when these are available only from
one source—is extremely questionable. On the evidence of complaints
received by the Office of Fair Trading, there is clearly no justification
for some of the things that go on. For example, the OFT has received
complaints relating to:

—a car manufacturer who does not supply spare ignition keys or
blanks—but only a lock-and-key set, at about twenty times the usual
cost of a key.

—a room heater whose impeller (fan mechanism) could be replaced
only as part of an assembly which included the fan motor and heater
element as well.

—an electrical circuit tester for which no replacement bulb was
available—and which therefore worked for only as long as the bulb
did.

On this and related evidence, it is clear that some producers deliberately aim to benefit from the exclusive sale of their components;
from the sale of more rather than less expensive parts; and also from
the rapid rate of obsolescence of their products. Most producers in
such a fortunate position (for them) will normally exercise some
discretion—consumer resistance being what it is. But there are still
outstanding instances when they do not.

Liability

The extent of a producer's after-sales responsibilities are determined
partly by discretion and custom, and partly by the producer's liability
in law.

It is largely left to producers to decide what arrangements are made
for the provision of service and spares. The producer's discretion is
generally relied on, because it is thought to be in his own best interests

(as well as everyone else's) if he provides at least an adequate after-sales service. However, in some industries (see checklist to this chapter) there also exist voluntary codes recommending minimum standards of after-sales service. The fact that such codes exist—and that the standard of compliance with them is often low[6]—must raise doubts either about the ability of some producers to serve their own best interests; or about where their best interests really lie; or perhaps about both.

Although retailers rather than producers are held legally liable for the provision of products of satisfactory quality—it is customary for many producers to guarantee the performance of their goods as well.

The existence of a guarantee guarantees nothing; its value depends entirely on what it says. Until recently, guarantees were often given in substitution for a purchaser's normal legal rights. However, since 1973,[7] anything offered in a guarantee (whatever rights it may purport to exclude) is given in addition to the consumer's normal rights against the supplier of the goods. These additional rights may or may not be worth having. If the guarantee gives cover for a reasonable period of time (normally one year) and provides for repair or replacement free of any charges for parts, labour and carriage, it is probably well worth having. On the other hand, it may not be worth (to the consumer) even the paper the guarantee is written on, if it includes restrictions of the following kind:

—Guarantee cover lasts for an unreasonably short period of time. (No minimum period is specified by law in any EEC country. Variations in the duration of guarantees may be found in identical products sold in different countries. *Social Audit on Avon* reported, for instance, that identical Avon inflatable craft are guaranteed for five years in the US, but for only one year in the UK.)

—Exclusion of liability for parts, labour or carriage, or of any liability for components in a product not made or supplied by the manufacturer issuing the guarantee. ('Some manufacturers disclaim all responsibility for components made by other firms . . .'[8])

—Attempted exclusion of purchasers' normal legal rights; and/or of the manufacturer's liability for negligence.

Consumers may also be put at a disadvantage (i) if guarantees apply only to the original purchaser, and are not transferable; (ii) if their validity is (said to be) conditional on the consumer completing and sending off to the manufacturer a 'guarantee registration card'. Such cards are often used by manufacturers for market research purposes, but may also adversely affect a consumer's legal rights; (iii) if the terms of the guarantee are not clearly expressed, and also displayed at the point of sale.

Legal liability for faults in goods can arise not only in (express or implied) contract, but also in reparation or tort. Under existing UK law, compensation for consequential loss, damage or personal injury may be obtained only if a consumer can prove that this was caused by negligence, usually on the manufacturer's part. In practice, it is extremely difficult, sometimes impossible, to do this—and many people have suffered severely, as a result.

However, at the time of writing (mid-1977), changes in the law seem likely soon to be made. Notably, a draft EEC directive (Com(76) 372 Final 23 July 1976) proposes to introduce 'no-fault' liability removing the need for the injured party to show that damage occurred through lack of due care by the producer. Though this could improve considerably on existing law, it would still leave some consumers unprotected in several important respects. In particular, though the burden of proof of fault is removed, the burden of proving the existence of a defect remains. This could present considerable difficulties—for example, when a product presumed to be defective is destroyed in the accident causing damage or loss; and/or in the absence of any right of complainants to get information which might enable them to prove a claim.

Prevention of loss

Leaving aside the issue of liability for *actual* loss, there is the important question of the producer's responsibility for preventing *possible* loss. This responsibility may be exercised by:

—informing consumers about the ways in which products should or should not be used, and warning them of any hazards which may exist if products are used in any way which might reasonably be foreseen;

—where defective goods—and particularly dangerous ones—are known to have been supplied, by warning consumers of the hazard by publicity or any other appropriate means; and by

—recalling stocks of those products, whether unsold or already in the hands of the public.

One important thing to appreciate is the actual level of ability of different people to understand information of different kinds; and/or to take appropriate actions in response. The 'functional competence' of a significant proportion of ordinary consumers is almost certainly far lower than is generally appreciated: for example, there are an estimated two million adults in the UK with a reading age below that of a nine-year-old—while 'functional literacy' is defined as the reading level of a 13-year old.[9] More detailed evidence of the same general kind (and with similar implications for producers) has been published in the US.[10]

Finally, there is the question of reporting and/or recalling defective or dangerous products. The conspicuous absence in UK law of any requirement either to notify an official agency, or otherwise to take corrective action, when serious product defects are known or suspected to exist—in one way actually emphasises the responsibilities that producers might assume. (On the other hand, the fact that many producers evidently ignore their responsibilities only underlines the inadequacy of the law.)

Reference has been made to the need for procedures to detect and remedy product defects in the checklist which follows.

Checklist on After-Sales

The following questions are intended both to summarise and amplify the main issues raised in the preceding chapter. They should be used in conjunction with the general questions relating to policy, organisation, procedures, resources and effects listed in Chapter 3 (pages 27 to 36); and also with the list of standards identified in Chapter 2 (pages 17 to 25).

Sales and after-sales
(1) Have satisfactory arrangements been made by the manufacturer, or on his behalf, for:

—inspection, testing, adjustment, etc. of the product immediately before sale and use?

—delivery times and methods?

—the assembly, installation or fitting of the product?

—consumer education or instruction—for example, relating to the use, service or repair of the product, or to complaints handling?

Comments
The consumer's right to receive products in good working order is enforceable against the retailer, whether or not the producer accepts liability himself. Normally such rights are given under the Sale of Goods Acts, but the provisions of the Trade Descriptions Act, Food and Drugs Act, Weights and Measures Act and the Fair Trading Act and other statutes may also apply (see note 1 on pages 24 to 25).

If arrangements are made between the producer and a distributor, retailer or other agent, whereby they undertake the inspection or adjustment of goods before sale, it would be important to check that it is appropriate that such work be delegated by the producer; that the agent is qualified to do such work; and is adequately rewarded for doing so. Any arrangement in which an agent is expected to perform work which might be done by the producer—and particularly where the agent's remuneration is relatively low—must be suspect.

Note that there is no requirement for producers to inform consumers how or where to complain about defective goods in any EEC country, other than Denmark.

Maintenance, service and repair

(2) Have satisfactory arrangements been made by the manufacturer, or on his behalf, for the maintenance, service or repair of products—and how do these:

—affect the dependence of the consumer on third parties for the diagnosis or correction of faults?
—affect the length of the useful life of products?
—affect the quality, availability or cost of servicing?
—affect the arrangements made for the settlement of disputes, through arbitration or other means?

(3) What arrangements have been made by the producer for:

—the appointment and training of service personnel, and for checking the adequacy of their work and their charges for it?
—giving information about the prevention of faults, and for their diagnosis and correction, both to consumers and to agents?
—collecting information from 'service returns' with a view to improving the design or manufacture of the product, and/or taking corrective action when substantial defects are found?
—providing an adequate network of service centres?

Comments

Several factors affecting the quality of service or repair were mentioned in the text. One which was not was the possibility of the producer either going out of business or being taken over. Both might affect the arrangements made for service or repair, and also the provision of spares and guarantees. In some service industries (travel or estate agency, for instance) insurance or bonding arrangements are made to protect consumers in the event of collapse. Could similar arrangements be made in manufacturing industries and, if not, what form of protection (if any) is given?

Both refilling and recharging might be considered under the general heading of servicing. Enquiries should be made to establish whether (loose or lightly packaged) refills are always available to consumers who have made an initial purchase of a product in a durable and reusable container.

Similarly, check all arrangements for reconditioning and recharging. It has been alleged that the 'reconditioning' of some electrical equipment in cars costs pounds, but involves little more than replacing the commutator brushes and then giving the equipment a good wipe or clean.

Another example: Eveready $1\frac{1}{2}$-volt transistor batteries sold in the US are labelled as guaranteed, unless the user tries to recharge the battery. But the equivalent Ever Ready battery, sold in the UK (which, despite the name, is made by a different firm) contains no such warning, nor a guarantee. However, the printed warnings on UK batteries used in flash guns and cine-cameras say that the batteries will explode if recharged—though some deny this is true. A contributor to the journal *Amateur Photographer*, for instance, has claimed (17 November 1976) that batteries can be safely recharged, provided a small current is used. He claimed to have got good service from one set of cine-camera batteries after 20 months' use and three re-chargings.

Criteria for judging the effectiveness of arrangements made for servicing (they relate, for instance, to speed of service, charges, supply of spares and protection of customers' property) are included in many codes of practice. Several major codes have been negotiated between the industries concerned and the Office of Fair Trading, since 1973. They include the AMDEA code of the Association of Manufacturers of Domestic Electrical Appliances, and codes administered by the National Association of Shoe Repair Factories, the Motor Agents Association, the Footwear Distributors Association and the Radio, Electrical and Television Retailers Association. In addition, there is the code of the Retail Trading Standards Association, and several British Standards also apply. (See BSI yearbook and/or BSI Sectional List No. 3, on consumer standards.) A few individual manufacturers (Currys Ltd, for example) have published their own codes as well.

Attention should be paid to arrangements for third-party servicing, and for servicing by consumers themselves. In some cases, manufacturers might provide consumer information—using manuals, or by training or demonstration. Similarly, arrangements might be made for consumers to report back to manufacturers or others, either on the adequacy of servicing arrangements and/or on product performance —particularly where major product defects or hazards were suspected or known.

Design, availability and cost of spares
(4) Has the manufacturer made satisfactory arrangements for:

—the standardisation and simplification of designs for spare parts ?
—the efficiency and extent of their distribution ?
—the length of time for which both functional and non-functional parts are stocked ?
—continuity of design in spare parts (to the greatest possible extent) despite changes in (successive models of) the product ?

Comments

Several of the codes referred to above include requirements for the stocking of spares—but they seem pretty feeble so far as they go, and they do not go further than that. Other, informal criteria have been suggested in the text, both in the preceding chapter and in Chapter 4 on Design.

We suggest enquiries are made not only about the terms on which spares are supplied to the manufacturer's own agents—but also about their supply to independents. In addition, it would be important to find out whether the manufacturer's tied outlets were free *not* to stock the company's own-brand spares.

How long should spares be kept and made available—and what effects does a company's stocking policies have on product life ? The industry codes mentioned above usually suggest that stocks should be held for a period of time equal to the expected life of the product, beyond the date when manufacture of the product stops. Other consumer bodies recommend that spares be kept for at least twice as long as this.

The life expectancy of consumer durables is not easy to assess, though it is elaborately defined. The 'expected life' of a product is generally taken to be :

> that period through which the product could be expected to give the service for which it was originally intended, to a reasonably satisfactory standard, taking account of the nature of the product and its construction and assuming that it has received throughout its life the normal use for which it was originally intended.
> (Currys Ltd, *A Statement of Trading Standards* (London : Currys Ltd, 1976), p. 15.)

Having said this, those codes which specify the life expectancy of different products do so by referring to average life. The AMDEA Code, for example, puts the life of different electrical products at between five and ten years (paragraph 5.3). However, as the following data from Papanek suggest, what products are built to do, what they do do, and what they can do—are three very different things. In *Design for the Real World* (London : Thames & Hudson, 1972, p. 30) Papanek includes the list below (for which unfortunately no explanation nor primary source is given[11]).

Product	Primary useful product life in years	Actual time used in US in years	Actual time used in under-developed countries in years
Bicycle	25	2	75
Washing machines and irons	5	5	25
Band-power tools	10	3	25
Automobiles	11	2.2	40+
Construction equipment	14	8	100+
General purpose industrial equipment	20	12	75+
Agricultural machinery	17	15	2500+
Railroad equipment	30	30	50+
Ships	30	15	80+
Miniaturised Hi-Fi photographic and film equipment	35	1.1	50

Provision and terms of guarantees

(5) In the provision of guarantees, are satisfactory arrangements made for:

—duration of cover?

—limitations of cover, assuming the product has been subject to normal use, which might affect component parts, charges made (for carriage, labour, for example) or transfer of product ownership?

—restriction of purchaser's or user's rights, or any attempted restriction of them?

—informing consumers of their rights under guarantee and drawing appropriate attention to any exclusions or limitations of rights?

—improving the terms of guarantees—whether this involves increasing the price of the product, or improving the standard of manufacture or design, or both?

—interpretation of the terms of the guarantee, and the settlement of any dispute arising over them?

Comments

No manufacturer is required to guarantee his products. Both the provision of a guarantee, and the terms on which it is given, depend on two main things. One is the market value of the guarantee (as a selling point) ; the other is the cost of honouring it (either by prevention or cure).

Some data on costs for several consumer durable products is given in the aforementioned study by the MIT Centre for Policy Alternatives, *The Productivity and Servicing of Consumer Durable Products*. The study suggests that, with some products, it will be more economical for a manufacturer who offers an extended guarantee to improve the reliability of the product, rather than simply to increase price, in order to absorb the increased costs of repair.

The study found, for example that the use of higher quality components might be justified in some equipment—because the longer the guarantee period, the higher the proportion of repair costs due to defective design. Reference is made to one study which showed that 90 per cent of the failures on colour-TV receivers, with 90-day warranties,ʻwere attributable to manufacturing or assembly errors— while, with a one-year warranty, 55 per cent of failures were due to faults in design.

In the light of that specific finding, it is worth noting that the Director of the UK Electronic Components Board has alleged that some UK component firms make parts for TVs in three different grades. Top quality components are made for the Japanese; second quality for West Germany; and third quality for the British. (Source: *Electrical and Radio Trading*, 18 March 1976, p. 7.)

Note that, in some cases, guarantees may be given but not advertised. For instance, in the UK tyre industry, most manufacturers say they 'stand by' their products but they do not advertise the fact, presumably because some consumers fail to appreciate their rights, and fail to take advantage of them.

Though statistics of claims made under guarantee may be misleading as indicators of product quality, or of what consumers pay for, they may be useful in determining (i) what consumers actually pay, regardless of what they get ; (ii) what total service costs are, in relation to total life-cycle costs ; (iii) the proportion of the service cost paid for by the consumer when purchasing the product ; and (iv) the effective useful life of the product.

These and other data might be analysed with a view to finding out what improvements there have been in product reliability ; what improvements have been or could be made in the terms of guarantees ; what reductions have occurred in the level of complaints ; what improvements have been made in product durability ; and what changes have occurred in charges for servicing and/or spares.

Loss prevention and compensation

(6) How satisfactory are the provisions made for the prevention of,

or compensation for, loss or damage associated with the use of the company's products, for example through :

—the provision of information at the time or point of sale, or thereafter ?
—measures taken to establish that such information is appreciated and acted on by consumers ?
—the collection and/or dissemination of information about safety-related and other defects known or suspected to exist ?
—arrangements for the freezing of stocks or recall, when serious defects are believed to exist ?
—provision of information relating to possible liability for damage or loss ?
—the extent and terms of any insurance cover relating to liability for damage or loss ?

Comments

It should be a fundamental requirement for any manufacturer to have an effective policy—relating to the prevention, correction and future prevention of serious product defects. The policy should apply to all concerned—in other words, the manufacturer and all his agents—and should, if possible, encourage the systematic reporting of suspected defects by consumers and all others concerned.

Even in the absence of any legal requirement for this (as in s.15(b) of the US Consumer Product Safety Act), it is essential that the company has developed plans for :

—the collection of data about actual and possible hazards both from within the organisation and from elsewhere ;
—informing senior management promptly of any hazards which do or may exist ;
—keeping records sufficient to identify the source, channels of distribution, and numbers of defective products involved ; and
—corrective actions, which might include the prevention of further distribution ; action to prevent continued or similar breakdowns ; alerting those already at risk ; and arranging for the recall of any products in use.

According to the US Consumer Product Safety Commission :

Experience has shown . . . that unless a formal policy for corrective action is implemented, the tendency exists only to pursue and correct the obvious, in an unorganised and incomplete manner. It has also been demonstrated that few aspects of the safety system

are more important, or have more substantive effect on the safety and integrity of the product, as well as the economics involved, than this component.
Handbook and Standard for Manufacturing Safer Consumer Products (Washington DC: CPSC, 1975, p. 27).

The less that is left to chance—in both preventing and correcting damage due to abnormal use or misuse of the product—then, within reason, the better things will be. Whether or not it is 'within reason' for producers to anticipate and allow for the possibility of damage depends on (i) how remote the possibilities of damage are; (ii) how damaging the effects are likely to be; and (iii) how easy or difficult it is to prevent damage taking place.

When assessing how remote the chances of something happening are, account must be taken of what people *do* do, rather than what they should do. Consumers do not generally make periodic checks on the wiring in electric plugs; they do not check the tyres on their cars daily before use; and they do not unplug their TV sets when they are not in use. Consumers never have and never will behave with the legendary caution and wisdom of 'the man on the Clapham omnibus'—and they should not be relied upon to do so.

9 The End Product

Taking a narrow view, the end product is simply the thing which is made and sold—a whole physical article which amounts to the sum of all or some of the parts already described. This end product, works as well as it is made to work; lasts so long as it is made to last; and to some extent probably sells as well as it is sold.

The end product is also what it is perceived to be. It can be described in terms of the use and pleasure that different articles do or do not bring. Many do find good uses and give great pleasure as well; but others do not and some indeed do catastrophic harm.

Finally, there is the end product which both symbolises and is symbolised by the consumer–producer relationship. This chapter is mostly concerned with that aspect.

The active-passive relationship

The relationship between consumers and producers is a function of the rights, powers and obligations of each. Those which apply to producers have already been discussed in detail—but what about the rights, obligations and powers of consumers?

All consumers have at least the right either to buy or not to buy: this is a fundamentally important right but, at the same time, not a very useful one. It certainly gives no entitlement to a fair deal: on the contrary, it extends to consumers the right to buy any bad, overpriced or dangerous product that can legally be offered for sale.

Neither does this right give individual consumers any significant power to directly influence the quality of the products they get. It simply allows consumers *not* to buy products—just as the ON/OFF switch on a television gives the individual viewer the power to avoid certain programmes, but no say in the TV station's programming.

In all, the simple right either to buy or not to buy has little practical significance. You might think it gives more or less compensation for the corresponding loss of freedom—the freedom to avoid endless and persis-

115

tent pressure to buy more and more and more. It is a major loss—in our view, too readily taken for granted.

An 'active' minority of consumers manage to extend these basic rights to their limits. They chose between products as carefully as they can; and they complain if they get less than they might have expected, or less than they had been led to expect. Individual consumers thereby have some power to reject unacceptable products—though mainly when these fall short of standards that producers have (or should have) set for themselves.

It is true that the collective actions of this minority—and those of the majority—will have some influence on what producers do. But this does not alter the fact that consumers generally play the passive role in a relationship which is worked actively, and to its furthest limits, on the producers' terms.

The really important rights that consumers have not been exacted from producers, by consumers succeeding in their roles as buyers. They have been given mainly as a result of the growing evidence of, and concern at, the failure of consumers to protect themselves—a failure which was inevitable, given the overwhelming obstruction and opposition put up by producers protecting their own.

The rights consumers have in law are therefore important not only for the protection they give. They are significant also for what they suggest about the true nature of the consumer–producer relationship—one in which the 'natural' rights of consumers are relatively very limited indeed.

Ironically, some of the main limitations on consumer rights have been justified in the name of 'consumer sovereignty'. The consumer is king, the argument goes. How can he get less than he deserves—unless through behaviour unbecoming to a king? If some consumers are stupid enough to buy bad products, or can afford to pay more than they should, then they probably deserve no better than they get. If virtue has its own reward, then idiocy and ignorance have theirs too.

This point of view is sometimes carried to extraordinarily unpleasant extremes. It was, for instance, by the manager of a US supermarket, in response to an enquiry from the local newspaper about his display of cans of what might have been a lethally contaminated soup. The coded serial numbers on these cans showed they came from a batch already implicated in a small but fatal outbreak of botulism poisoning and, incidentally, subject to the manufacturer's recall. The manager was quoted in the newspaper, saying: 'We've been debating on whether to remove the soup . . . but we figure the serial number has been published. And if people are dumb enough to buy it . . . that's their problem'.[1]

It would be wrong to suggest that most people would go to such extremes. But are they not going in the same direction, and with much the same 'justification' for doing so? Or is it the case, as one distinguished consumer advocate has suggested, that 'the great crime against the consumer in this country is inefficiency'[2]—and not much more than that?

It is not only vital to know which; it is vital also to know the extent of the damage done. The fact that we do not know either only under-lines the need for business accountability, whether by social audits or by other means.

What goes wrong?

Whatever the reason, such evidence as there is clearly indicates that consumers frequently get much less than is either promised, expected or due—and it follows that producers almost certainly get much more. The evidence is far from complete: government has only just seriously begun to accumulate information on this, and much of the information there is is never published at all.

The hardest published evidence comes from the Office of Fair Trading,[3] which classifies and records complaints received from trading standards departments, and from Citizens' Advice Bureaux and other sources as well. Complaints run to about half a million a year; and cover the following goods, services and trading practices (Tables 6 and 7).

Many more complaints are made to other organisations—for example, to consumer bodies, to retailers or to the manufacturers themselves—and there are likely to be an even greater number never made at all.

The fact a complaint is not made obviously does not mean that grounds for complaints do not exist. The absence of complaint may mean either that grounds for grievance have not been perceived; or that a grievance has not been pursued.

Grounds for grievance

There are two main reasons why grounds for grievance may not be perceived. Consumers may not appreciate that a product has a fault; and they may not appreciate who is responsible for that fault.

A 'fault' may not be recognised because it is not related to mal-function, or because it is relatively very small. If, for example, a million people every day spend a halfpenny more than they should on a product, their individual loss will be small—but the producer will gain to the extent of £1½ million a year. (Some of this, typically, would be ploughed back into advertising and other persuasions, to suggest that a marginally extra cost would be worth paying for a mightily better product.)

Then what may be recognised as a deficiency in a product, may not be perceived as the product's fault. For instance, parents universally despair of children who are 'hard on their shoes'. Children may be hard on their shoes—but everyone *expects* them to be, including manufacturers who are obliged to sell goods which are fit for the purpose for which they are intended to be used. It is likely that some of the fault lies with manufacturers, even if it is not appreciated as such.

Table 6

CONSUMER COMPLAINTS
ANALYSED BY TRADING PRACTICES

	Incidence as % of total
Offers of inadequate redress	14
Imposition of unreasonable restrictions on consumers	7
Complaints about the manner in which prices and other conditions are communicated	1
Complaints about price comparisons	1
General price complaints	8
Inadequate information about the terms of a contract	1
Complaints about deceptive statements to consumers	1
Complaints about selling methods (not included above)	1
Practices in connection with packaging	1
Other practices affecting consumers' economic interests	17
Practices affecting or likely to affect consumers' health and safety	1
Other trading practices which consumers find objectionable	1
Complaints relating to lack of consumer information	2
Complaints about credit not covered by legislation	1
Goods not of merchantable quality or fit for their purpose	23
Failure to deliver goods, services or facilities ordered or promised	5
Other breach of contract cases	4
Complaint adequately covered by Trade Descriptions Act 1968	7
Complaint adequately covered by existing criminal sanction	6
Complaint adequately covered by existing Consumer Credit Act 1974	1

Table 7

CONSUMER COMPLAINTS
ANALYSED BY GOODS AND SERVICES

	Incidence as % of total
Food and drink	8
Footwear	5
Clothing and textiles	10
Furniture and floor covering	10
Household appliances	13
Toilet requisites, soaps, detergents, etc.	1
Toys, games, sports goods, etc.	1
Solid and liquid fuels	2
Motor vehicles and accessories	13
Other consumer goods	10
Non-consumer goods	1
Land, including houses	1
Construction	2
Repairs and servicing to domestic electrical appliances (excluding radio and TV)	1
Repairs and servicing to motor vehicles	2
Other repairs and servicing	3
Cleaning	1
Public utilities and transport	3
Consumer credit	1
Entertainment and accommodation	1
Holidays	1
Professional services	2
Special offers	1
General services, etc.	4

One of the main grounds for complaint is knowledge of the existence (or possibility) of a superior product—available at a comparable price, or which gives considerably better value. Without this knowledge, many conspicuous and other faults may simply be regarded as part of some natural order of things. For instance, until the recent introduction of sugarless chewing gum, many chewers probably thought more about the prospects of losing their teeth, than about the possibility of the product being modified to avoid doing such harm.

Equally, how could consumers be expected to appreciate something like the following case of 'planned obsolescence':

The filament of a GLS (General Lighting Service) light may be coiled once ('single-coil'), or more compactly twice ('coiled-coil').

Single-coil lamps stand up better to vibration and shock, and are preferable for industrial use; coiled-coil lamps are about 10 per cent more efficient, and are preferable for domestic and commercial use. Doubling lamp life is merely a matter of increasing the length and diameter of the filament by 5.4 per cent and 1.6 per cent respectively, thereby reducing its temperature sufficiently to halve evaporation; the resulting lamp costs 1 per cent more to make, and is 7.6 per cent less efficient.

For many years, the industry would only supply 1000-hour lamps, arguing that the lower efficiency associated with a longer life would have the net effect of increasing the average user's total costs, an argument which has always been generally accepted (although in fact fallacious). At the same time, it had to make a range of voltage ratings, including 250V lamps, because 240V supplies were not then universal. Now, 250V, 1000-hour lamps are in fact 240V, 1800-hour lamps with a different marking; their employment as such—'under-running'—was limited by user ignorance on the one hand, and by fallacious cost comparisons on the other . . .[4]

The extent and consequences of consumers' lack of experience or expertise may be alarming—as the following example shows, in relation to the safety and efficiency of proprietary drugs.

The Sainsbury Committee, in 1967, was neither the first nor last authority to comment on this issue, but they had formidable evidence in support of their conclusions.[5] Briefly, the Committee invited two distinguished panels of independent experts to assess the therapeutic effectiveness of 2657 preparations. The panels, who worked independently, totally agreed about the classification of 2241 drugs—84.3 per cent of the total. These preparations were classified as follows:

Effective drugs, whose therapeutic effectiveness depends on a single chemical substance	50 per cent
Rational combinations: that is, preparations containing more than one effective drug, the combination of which is rational	8 per cent
Not yet classifiable: drugs and preparations which are pharmacologically active but which are of unproven therapeutic value or safety or about which too little is known	7 per cent
Undesirable preparations, including (i) preparations containing more than one drug in combinations which are irrational, (ii) superseded or obsolete drugs or preparations; and (iii) ineffective drugs and preparations	35 per cent

The fact that one-third or more of the drugs made available by pharmaceutical companies are officially considered to be undesirable is alarming. The fact that their existence is encouraged by the prescribing habits of supposedly highly trained and motivated consumers (such as doctors) is perhaps more alarming still. The extent to which comparable situations exist elsewhere is not known—but, on the evidence of this drug study, the implications are clear enough.

In particular, there may be serious problems with product safety. The range and complexity of many actual and potential product hazards is such that consumers cannot possibly be expected to anticipate them. This is especially so with chronic or latent injuries, and more likely when these arise from an unexpected source. Recent examples involve mutagenic hair dyes, fabric conditioners which may exacerbate bronchial asthma, and soft-toy fillings which release cyanide gases if they smoulder or burn.[6]

Grievances not pursued

Alternatively, grievances may be felt, but not formally pursued.

This would be characteristic when the losses involved are relatively small. The relationship between extent of loss and incidence of complaint is not exactly known—but pilot data from the Office of Fair Trading suggests, not surprisingly, that complaints are more likely to be made when worth making:

> The results of the survey showed that whilst 40 per cent of the goods complained of cost less than £20, the average cost was £90. The average cost of making a complaint, taking into account time spent, cost of 'phone calls, letters, etc. was just under £8.[7]

Other reasons for not complaining would include feeling either foolish, or forgiving.[8] In addition, consumers may find fault, but not think it worth complaining—and may well be right. For instance, many people positively dislike certain advertising and promotional techniques—but live with them rather than formally complain.[9]

However, people may not know how to complain effectively, or to whom. A survey of consumer 'types' carried out in 1976 by the EEC distinguished between the kinds of people more and less likely to complain. At one end of the scale was the 12 per cent of hostile and critical folk, who could certainly be relied on to complain. At the other extreme were three groups of people considered unlikely or unable to do so. They included (a) the 'indifferent'—8 per cent of the total sample, who tended to live in rural areas, have little formal education and low incomes; (b) the 'careless'—8½ per cent of the total—who were characterised by not checking prices, weights or labels, nor the change in their final bill; and (c) the 9 per cent identified as not 'very earnest' and 'rather confused'. These three unfortunately labelled groups—representing one-quarter of all consumers—would be particularly unlikely to complain, or be able to do so to good effect.[10]

Against this, it may be argued that often the most 'telling' and appropriate complaint a consumer can make is not to buy an offending brand, but to buy a rival one. If a good alternative brand is available and if the consumer is aware of it, this may well be true.

But how often is this the case? The examples of light bulbs and proprietary medicines—two among many—suggest that producers can persist in malpractice, either withholding or distorting their information as it suits them to do so. As the tobacco industry demonstrates, in its steadfast refusal to accept overwhelming objective evidence of the damage that smoking does, these people have to believe what they say themselves, in order to believe in themselves.

If these producers cannot do otherwise, when the public interest clearly dictates they should, perhaps they should forfeit the power to do what they want. At least, so long as society entrusts them with power, it cannot, or must not, abdicate its own responsibility to call them to account.

Last complaint of all

It would be only fair to acknowledge in conclusion that consumers who have, have much to be thankful for—for the benefits and pleasure that good goods undoubtedly may bring.

If consumers do not always recognise these benefits and feel such pleasure, it is not simply through ingratitude or greed. For the system in which we are involved itself promotes the instinct and the will to complain, and provides unending grounds for dissatisfaction. If it did not—if people were ever allowed to be satisfied with what they had—then they would not want to buy and buy, and in time the system would falter and fail.

It is true that dissatisfaction may be a driving force for progress—and also for what passes for it—but the notion that we can make real progress by making dissatisfaction is very hard to swallow.

To take the widest view, to be part of a system which does so much to contrive dissatisfaction, in order to market palliative products to the few—in a world in which consumption for most means the salvage of human dignity, if not life and death—seems as fundamentally wrong as anything possibly could be.

Text References

Preface

1. For example, out of a group of 40 middle managers questioned by the author in the course of a business school seminar (1976) only seven said they thought the public would be reassured if they really knew what went on in business. See also: Simon Webley, *Towards a Code of Business Ethics* (London: Christian Association of Business Executives, 1972).

1   Power and Responsibility in Business

1. Robert A. Dahl, 'Governing the Giant Corporation', in Ralph Nader and Mark J. Green (eds.), *Corporate Power in America* (New York: Grossman, 1973), p. 11.

2. Richard C. Gerstenberg, Chairman of General Motors Corporation, quoted in John Humble, *Social Responsibility Audit* (London: Foundation for Business Responsibilities, 1973), p. 24.

3. Robert A. Dahl, op. cit. p. 11.

4. J. K. Galbraith, 'On the Economic Image of Corporate Enterprise', in Ralph Nader and Mark J. Green (eds.), *Corporate Power in America* (New York: Grossman, 1973), p. 4.

5. This account is adapted from data published in US *Consumer Reports;* and in *New York Times* (Business and Finance section, 23 November 1976).

6. Lucy Hodges and Charles Medawar, 'Advertising: the Art of the Permissible', in *Social Audit* No. 5, p. 30.

2   Standards

1. There is considerable evidence of this. See, for example, Owen A. Hartley, 'Inspectorates in British Central Government', *Public Administration* (Winter 1972), pp. 447–66. Also see: Maurice Frankel 'The Alkali Inspectorate', *Social Audit* (Spring 1974)—and numerous Nader Study Group publications (list available from Center for Study of Responsive Law; see p. 140).

123

2. Regulations made under the Food And Drugs Act 1955.

3. *Annual Report of the Director General of Fair Trading* (London: HMSO, 1977).

4. See Lucy Hodges and Charles Medawar, 'The Social Cost of Advertising' and 'Advertising: the Art of the Permissible' in *Social Audit* No. 1 and No. 5 (Summer 1973 and Summer 1974, respectively).

5. Geoffrey Chandler, a director of Shell International, reported in *The Guardian* (5 January 1973).

6. *Company Law Reform*, Cmnd. 5391 (London: HMSO, 1973).

7. Gordon Borrie and Aubrey L. Diamond, *The Consumer, Society and the Law*, 3rd ed. (Harmondsworth: Penguin, 1973), p. 138.

8. ITT Europe Inc. *ITT in Europe* (Brussels: ITT, December 1974), p. 2; and Anthony Sampson, *The Sovereign State* (London: Coronet, 1974).

9. For further information, see Borrie and Diamond, op. cit. pp. 148–51.

3 Information

1. J. Melrose-Woodman and I. Kverndal, *Towards Social Responsibility —Company Codes of Ethics and Practice* (London: British Institute of Management, 1976).

2. *Guardian* (25 November 1975) on the report on *John Willment Automobiles Ltd:* Investigation under section 165b of the Companies Act 1948, reported by P. J. Millett QC and M. R. Harris FCA, inspectors appointed by the Department of Trade. (London: HMSO, 1975).
The alleged offences by the Company were essentially 'technical'— relating mainly to reporting requirements under company law.

3. Quoted in 'The First Social Audit: Tube Investments Ltd', *Social Audit* No. 3, p. 9.

4. Community Action, *Investigator's Handbook* (P.O. Box 665, London SW1X 8DZ, undated); Labour Research Department, *How to Get the Facts about Prices and Profits* (London: LRD Publications, 1975); and Christopher Hird, *Your Employer's Profits* (London: Pluto Press, 1975).

5. These standards referred to in: Comptroller General of the United States, *Standards for the Audit of Governmental Organisations, Programs, Activities and Functions* (Washington DC: US General Accounting Office, 1972), pp. 13–20.

6. Roy Jenkins (in oral evidence) in *Report of the Departmental Committee on Section 2 of the Official Secrets Act 1911* (London: HMSO, 1972), Vol. 4, p. 374.

7. (Washington DC: US General Accounting Office, 1972).

4 Design

1. An introduction to the Corporate Plan may be obtained from E. F. Scarbrow, Secretary, Lucas Aerospace Combine, Shop Stewards Committee, 86 Mellow Lane East, Hayes, Middlesex.

2. See, for example: Victor Papanek, *Design for the Real World* (London: Thames and Hudson, 1972). It is well worth reading, and has a useful bibliography with over 500 titles.

3. To take an extreme but not unusual case, a group of UK employees would be poorly placed in bargaining for improvements in average UK working conditions, if they were competing directly with firms employing sweated labour overseas. The UK employees could not compete in the absence of outright protection, as might be provided by import controls. (Anti-dumping measures might give some protection only if externalised costs—such as accidents to workers or pollution—were treated universally as part of the true cost of production.)

4. Victor Papanek, op. cit., p. 9.

5. H. J. H. Starks and R. D. Lister, *Some Safety Aspects of Pedal and Motor-Assisted Cycles* (London: Road Research Laboratory, Technical Paper No. 38, 1957).

6. Raymond Baxter (Presenter) *Tomorrow's World* (BBC Television programme transmitted 10 June 1976).

7. House of Lords Official Report; Vol. 356, No. 49 (19 February 1975). Col. 287.

8. T. P. Hoar (Chairman) *Report of the Committee on Corrosion and Protection* (London: HMSO for the Department of Trade and Industry, 1971), p. 21.

9. In late 1977, Uniroyal Ltd introduced its air deflector—an add-on device which aims to reduce this problem. And, at the time of going to press, there were found to be other competing brands on the market as well.

10. This point is developed by attorneys Harry M. Philo and Arnold D. Portner in an article in the November 1976 issue of *Trial*, journal of the American Trial Lawyers Association. The authors suggest: 'Thousands of deaths and tens of thousands of injuries each year are doubtless attributable to defective tires'. They are reported as saying that 'lack of sophistication in tire technology by accident reconstructionists and attorneys representing injured parties has failed to reveal the alarming magnitude of the hazard' (*Washington Star*, 5 November 1976).

11. US Department of Labor press release dated 4 November 1976.

12. Several different specifications may exist for any one product. A specification may be 'a user's description to a designer of his requirements for purpose or duty; it may be a designer's description to a manufacturer, or an embodiment of those requirements; or it may be a manufacturer's detailed description to his operator of the components, materials, methods, etc. necessary to achieve that embodiment; or it may be a statement by a seller describing suitability for purpose to satisfy a need, or even a potential need, of a user or possible user. It may of course be all or some of these in one'.—British Standards Institution, *Guide to the Preparation of Specifications* (London: BSI, 1967).

13. There is no reason in principle why consumer agencies should not be given equal access to such essential information—but, perhaps for want of asking, they generally are not. On what grounds could such a request *reasonably* be refused of a body representing possibly hundreds of thousands of consumers—when a manufacturer would willingly meet such a request from a single buyer with only a fraction of that purchasing power?

14. Monopolies Commission, *Household Detergents* (London: House of Commons Paper 105, 1966).

15. Center for Policy Alternatives and Charles Stark Draper Laboratory Inc., *The Productivity and Servicing of Consumer Durable Products* (Center for Policy Alternatives, MIT, Report No. CPA-74-4, 1974), pp. 116–7.

16. Office of Fair Trading, *Beeline* (No. 2, 1975). Complaints coded as K1, K4, K7, K8 and K9.

17. T. A. B. Corley, *Domestic Electrical Appliances* (London: Cape, 1966), p. 113.

5 Manufacture and Quality Control

1. Spot welder at the Ford assembly plant in Chicago, quoted by Studs Terkel in *Working* (Chicago: Avon, 1975).

2. Preamble to the section on 'Manufacturing Control: General', from *Quality Control System Requirement for Industry* (Ministry of Defence Standard 05-21/Issue 1; 1973).

3. Ministry of Defence, *Quality Control System Requirements for Industry*, op. cit., p. 3.

4. US Consumer Product Safety Commission, *Handbook and Standards for Manufacturing Safer Consumer Products* (Washington DC: Consumer Product Safety Commission, June 1975), pp. 12–13.

5. An example of this being car tyre failure, referred to in note 10, Chapter 4, above.

6. Colin Greenhalgh, *Financial Times* (27 February 1975), p. 21.

7. Alisdair Aird, *The Automotive Nightmare* (London: Hutchinson 1972), p. 32.

8. Sir Eric Mensforth (Chairman), *Report of a Committee on the Means of Authenticating the Quality of Engineering Products and Materials* (London: HMSO, for the Department of Trade and Industry, 1971), p. 41.

9. Among others, Professor J. Loxham of the Unit of Precision Engineering at *Cranfield Institute of Technology* has proposed a government-backed 'quality assurance service' (source: John Langley, *Daily Telegraph*, 21 April 1976, p. 12).

6 Packaging and Labelling

1. Impressive evidence of the disproportionate extra cost of small packs may be found, for example, in Price Commission Report No. 21, *The Unit Prices of Small Packs* (London: HMSO, 1976).

2. See 'The Impulse Buyers' in the *Sunday Times* (25 July 1976), p. 41. This is a brief report on the 1976 survey 'How Housewives Really Shop', carried out by the market research firm, Business Decisions Ltd, and available through *Marketing* magazine.

3. See: *Secret Remedies* (1909) and *More Secret Remedies* (1912)—both published by the British Medical Association, and both classics in consumer protection.

4. National Electronic Injury Surveillance System, *NEISS News* (Washington DC: Consumer Product Safety Commission, March 1976).

5. Price Commission, *Fruit and Vegetables, Interim Report* (London: HMSO, 1974).

6. Caroline Moorehead in *The Times* (10 April 1974).

7. Maureen Walker in the *Sunday Times* (20 October 1974).

8. Price Commission 1976; op. cit.

9. For example: Friends of the Earth, *Packaging in Britain* (London: FOE, 1973).

7 Marketing and Competition

1. Cape (London 1977).

2. (September 1972).

3. Peter Blood, 'Good Manners for Marketers' in supplement to *Marketing* (April 1976).

4. Fair Trading Act 1973. Part One, Section 2(1)(a).

5. Retail Trading Standards Association, *Trading Standards in a Nutshell* (London: RTSA, 1968, under revision, 1977–78).

8 After-sales

1. See *Euroforum*, No. 18/76 (4 May 1976), Annex 1, p. 1 reporting on a BEUC survey of after-sales service in EEC countries.

2. *Which?* (February 1977), p. 61.

3. Alisdair Aird, op. cit., p. 32.

4. *Practical Householder* (September 1976).

5. Center for Policy Alternatives, *The Productivity and Servicing of Consumer Durable Products*, op. cit. pp. 75–85.

6. For example, see *Which?* (February 1977) pp. 61–65.

7. Under the *Supply of Goods (Implied Terms) Act 1973*, attempted exclusions of purchasers' normal legal rights are void. But it is not illegal (nor uncommon) for a guarantee to contain conditions which might mislead consumers into believing they have lost such rights. In addition, the Unfair Contract Terms Act 1977 makes ineffective any clause which a firm may use to try and exclude or limit its liability for death or injury caused by its negligence. Also, clauses relating to exclusions for other loss or damage caused through negligence will be effective only if a firm can convince a court that the clause is 'reasonable'.

8. *Which?* (April 1976), p. 78.

9. This is the definition of 'functional literacy' used by UNESCO. See *Legal Action Group Bulletin* (February 1977), p. 31.

10. University of Texas at Austin, Division of Extension, Dr. W. E. Barron, Dean. *Adult Functional Competency: A Summary*, March 1975.

11. This is disturbing, because some of the data in this Table really need to be explained. For instance, miniaturised Hi-Fi, photographic and film equipment has not been available for 50 years—which is said to be the *actual* time they have been used in under-developed countries.

9 The End Product

1. *Consumer Reports* (November 1971), p. 646 (quoting from *The Charlotte (NC) Observer*.

2. Dame Elizabeth Ackroyd, in 'Value for Money', *Study on Three* (BBC Radio 3 broadcast, 4 January 1971).

3. Details of complaints have been published in the OFT newsletter, *Beeline*. The data here has been extrapolated from returns of complaints for the period April to June, 1976.

4. I. D. M. Meiklejohn, *Restrictive Agreements in the British Lamp Industry, with particular reference to the Durability of Discharge Lamps* (unpublished paper, dated 13 December 1976).

5. Lord Sainsbury (Chairman), *Report of the Committee of Enquiry into the Relationship of the Pharmaceutical Industry with the National Health Service*, Cmnd 3410 (London: HMSO, 1967).

6. These and other examples appeared in press and media reports between 1974 and 76—and were all reported in Consumers' Association's *Daily Consumer News Sheet*.

7. Office of Fair Trading, *Beeline* No. 5 (December 1976), p. 5.

8. 'Why victims of shoddy repairs don't complain', in *New Society* (13 May 1976).

9. Evidence of this may be found in the survey *The General Public's Attitude to Advertising* (London: Advertising Association, July 1972); *Public Attitudes to Advertising* (London: Advertising Association, 1976); and *1976 Review* (London: Harris International Shopping and Promotion Intelligence, 1976). All indicate that significant minorities positively dislike much advertising and many promotion techniques.

10. *Sunday Times* (Business News 18 July 1976).

Part Three—Appendix

We hope this book will encourage further enquiry and action. To this end, we are including notes on sources of reference material and further reading, and on relevant organisations and institutions. Our main aim has been to suggest where and how to get information, rather than to recommend individual sources. See also the note about *Public Interest Research Centre Ltd.* and *Social Audit*, on pages v and 144 to 148.

Reference materials and further reading

If you intend to make a comprehensive literature search—for example, to do exhaustive research in some area—then you should follow the detailed procedures explained in specialised publications in library science (for example, in the *Introductory Guide to Research* mentioned in the reading list for Chapter 3, below). For most purposes, however, go to a main reference library, where the appropriate directories (or staff) will suggest sources of bibliographies and abstracts. These will help identify the specific publications you may need.

You may want access to a specialised library. The main ones are listed (and information about their holdings given) in such publications as: *Guide to Government and other Libraries and Information Bureaux; Inventory of Bibliographic Data Bases Produced in the UK;* or *Industrial and Related Library and Information Services in the UK* (see reading list for Chapter 3, below).

There are numerous directories and reference guides, far too may to list. As a starting point, try any one of the guides mentioned in the reading list for Chapter 3, below—or a more general publication, such as *Current British Directories* (Beckenham, Kent: CBD Ltd).

There are also many bibliographies and abstracting services; and a number of guides to them. Two useful guides are *Ulrich's International Periodicals Directory* and *Irregular Serials and Annuals—an International*

Directory: see entries under 'Abstracting and Indexing Services' and 'Bibliographies'. In addition, it may be worth approaching appropriate organisations for bibliographical or abstracted material. One reason for doing this is to get up-to-date material; another is to locate materials which are not published, but which are prepared essentially for in-house use. (For example, Consumers' Association maintains its *Index to Overseas Consumer Reports* on card file. Similarly, we found no reference to *CA's Daily Consumer News Sheet* in the standard directories—though it is probably the UK's principal consumer abstract service—prepared mainly for the use of CA staff, but available elsewhere.)

There are several one-off bibliographies on consumer and related issues, for example, the *Consumer Bibliography* published by the Office of Fair Trading (Susan Samuel, 1976) and *A Bibliography of Recent Consumerism Literature* (preliminary version by Folke Ölander and Håkan Lindhoff, International Institute of Management, Berlin, July 1973). The HMSO Sectional List No. 3, includes recent government publications on Trade, Industry, Energy and Prices and Consumer Protection, which may be useful.

Anyone familiar with these or other bibliographies will recognise that the titles listed below—in addition to those cited in the text references, pages 123 to 129, are a very small proportion of the total. Some other publications (particularly periodicals) have been identified in the section on Organisations and Institutions, pages 138 to 144.

Chapter 1

Subject/search headings: business, for example, social responsibilities of; *consumerism*, for example, influence on business; *management*, for example, decision-making processes; *government*, for example, regulation of business; *politics* and *economics*, for example, competition, control of business activity.

Ralph Nader (ed.) *The Consumer and Corporate Accountability* (New York: Harcourt Brace Jovanovich, 1973).

Ralph Nader and Mark J. Green (eds.) *Corporate Power in America* (New York: Grossman, 1973).

Raymond A. Bauer and Dan H. Fenn Jr., *The Corporate Social Audit* (New York: The Russell Sage Foundation, 1972).

Meinolf Dierkes and Raymond A. Bauer (eds.) *Corporate Social Accounting* (New York: Praeger, 1973).

Neil H. Jacoby, *Corporate Power and Social Responsibility* (London: Collier-Macmillan, 1973).

Edmond Marquès, *Taking into Account the Economic and Social Responsibility of the Firm* (Paper published by Centre d'Enseignement Superior des Affairs, 1 Rue de la Liberation, 78 Jouy-en-Josas, France, 1975).

David A. Aaker and George S. Day (eds.) *Consumerism* (New York: The Free Press, 1971).

International Labour Organisation, *Study Guide on Consumer Protection* (Geneva: ILO, 1976).

J. T. Molony QC (Chairman), *Final Report of the Committee on Consumer Protection*, Cmnd. 1781 (London: HMSO, 1963).

Folke Ölander and Håkan Lindhoff, *Consumer Action Research: A Review of the Consumerism Literature and Suggestions for New Directions in Theoretical and Empirical Research* (Berlin: International Institute of Management, 1974).

OECD Committee on Consumer Policies, *Annual Reports on Consumer Policy in OECD Countries* (Paris: Organisation for Economic Cooperation and Development, annual).

Central Office of Information, *Fair Trading and Consumer Protection in Britain*, COI Reference Pamphlet No. 144 (London: HMSO, 1976).

Consumer Information Center, General Services Administration, *Consumer Information* (Washington DC: U.S. Government Printing Office, quarterly).

Office of Consumer Affairs, *Directory of Consumer Organisations: A Selected Listing of Non-Government Organisations at Local, State and National Levels* (Washington DC: U.S. Department of Health, Education and Welfare, 1976).

Chapter 2

Subject/search headings: laws, standards, codes of practice, regulation, purchasing and contracting, testing, etc.

G. Borrie and A. L. Diamond, *The Consumer, Society and the Law* (Harmondsworth: Penguin, 1973).

National Press Commission (Occasional Paper No. 9) *Consumer Protection Law in America, Canada and Europe* (Dublin: Dublin Stationery Office, 1973).

Department of Prices and Consumer Protection, *Register of Test Houses* (London: DPCP, 1976).

International Organisation for Standardisation, *Memento* (Geneva: ISO, annual).

British Standards Institution, *Yearbook* (London: BSI, annual).

National Technical Information Service, *Guide to Standards Activities of Federal Agencies* (Springfield Va.: U.S. Department of Commerce, 1976).

Ministry of Defence, *Index of Defence Publications* (London: MOD, 1976), 9th ed.

Peter Baily and David Farmer, *Purchasing Principles and Techniques* (London: Pitman, for the Institute of Purchasing and Supply, 1974).

Russell F. Settle and Burton F. Weisbrod, *Governmentally Imposed*

Standards: Some Normative and Positive Aspects (Madison, Wis.: University of Wisconsin, Department of Economics, 1976).

Rt. Hon. Sir David Renton (Chairman), *The Preparation of Legislation*, Cmnd. 6053 (London: HMSO, 1975).

Colin Turpin, *Government Contracting* (Harmondsworth: Penguin, 1972).

Consumer Protection Committee, *Consumer Code* (Manchester: Co-operative Union, 1976).

Chapter 3

Subject/search headings: information, accounting, accountability, research, investigation, secrecy, reference, directories and *guides.*

Patricia Ward *et al.* (eds.) *Introductory Guide to Research in Library and Information Studies in the UK* (London: Library Association, 1975).

Library Association, *Guide to Reference Material*, Vol. 1, Science and Technology; Vol. 2, Social and Historical Sciences, etc. (London: Library Association, 1975).

British Library Lending Division, *Guide to British Reports, Translations and Theses* (Boston Spa, Yorks.: BLLD Announcement Bulletin, 'published regularly').

Library Association, *Guide to Current British Journals* (London: Library Association, 1975).

Science Reference Library, *Guide to Government Department and other Libraries and Information Bureaux* (London: Science Reference Library, 1976).

British Library (Research and Development Report No. 5256), *Inventory of Bibliographic Data Bases produced in the UK* (London: British Library, 1976).

Government Statistical Office, *Government Statistics: A Brief Guide to Sources* (London: HMSO, 1977).

Library Association, *Recommended Basic Statistical Sources: International* (London: Library Association, 1975).

Library Association, *Industrial and Related Library and Information Sources in the UK* (London: Library Association, 1972).

National Council of Social Service, *CANS* (Citizens' Advice Notes: 'A service of information compiled from authoritative sources' including sections on business and industry, local government, public health, administration of justice, etc.); (London: NCSS, annual).

Maxine MacCafferty (Compiler) *A Right to Know*, ASLIB Bibliography No. 1 (London: ASLIB, 1976).

James Michael with Ruth Fort (eds.) *Working the System: A Comprehensive Manual for Citizen Access to Federal Agencies* (New York: Basic Books, 1974).

Jean Atkinson, *A Handbook for Interviewers* (London: HMSO, 1971).

L. C. J. McNae (ed.) *Essential Law for Journalists* (London: Staples Press, 1975).

Ulrich's *International Periodicals Directory*, 16th ed., 1975–76; and *Irregular Serials and Annuals*, 4th ed., 1976–77 (London: Bowker, 1976).

Roy Manley and Helen Hastings, *Influencing Europe: A Guide for Pressure Groups* (London: Fabian Society, 1977).

Chapter 4

Subject/search headings: design (theory, practice and techniques), *innovation, product development, consumer research,* etc.

Victor Papanek, *Design for the Real World* (London: Thames and Hundson, 1972). Also, *How Things Don't Work* (New York: Pantheon Books, 1977).

Design and Industries Association, *Design Action* (London: Design and Industries Association, annual).

Andrew Robertson, *Lessons of Failure: Cases and Comments on Consumer Product Innovation* (London: MacDonald, 1974).

Roderick White, *Consumer Product Development* (Harmondsworth: Pelican, 1976).

The New Implications and Responsibilities of Design (London: Industrial and Commercial Techniques Ltd, 1973).

Folke Ölander and Håkan Lindhoff, *The Influence of Consumers on the Development of New Products* (Berlin: International Institute of Management, 1973).

Barry Commoner, *The Poverty of Power* (London: Cape, 1977).

Georgia Institute of Technology, *Technical Innovation: A Critical Review of Current Knowledge* (Washington DC: National Science Foundation, 1975).

Chapter 5

Subject/search headings: manufacture, production, quality control, record keeping, etc. Readers are advised to refer to specialised texts (such as on injection-moulding, polymer technology, food science, etc.) as appropriate.

British Institute of Management, *Production Management, Production Planning* and *Quality Control* (Reading Lists) (London: BIM, 1976).

British Institute of Management, *Decision Making* (Checklist) (London: BIM, 1973).

H. B. Maynard, *Handbook of Modern Manufacturing Management* (1970); J. H. Greene, *Production and Inventory Control* (1970); W. G. Ireson, *Reliability Handbook* (1966); J. M. Juran, *Quality Control Handbook* (1974) (Maidenhead, Berks.: McGraw-Hill).

Chapter 6

Subject/search headings: packaging, containers, labelling, information, waste disposal, etc.

National Federation of Consumer Groups, *Survey Reports on Packaging* (Birmingham; NFCG, 1976).

British Institute of Management, *Packaging* (Checklist) (London: BIM, 1973).

National Business Council for Consumer Affairs, Subcouncil on Product Safety, *Guiding Principles for Responsible Packaging and Labelling* (Washington DC: U.S. Government Printing Office, 1972).

J. R. Hanlon, *Handbook of Package Engineering* (Maidenhead, Berks.: McGraw-Hill, 1971).

G. S. Brady and H. Clauser, *Materials Handbook* (Maidenhead, Berks.: McGraw-Hill, 1977).

Friends of the Earth, *Material Gains: Reclamation, Recycling and Reuse* (London: FOE, 1975).

Metal Containers in the Environment—working party on the design, use and disposal of metal containers (London: British Tin Box Manufacturers' Federation, 1973).

John P. Liefeld, *European Informative Labelling* (Ottawa: Department of Consumer and Corporate Affairs, 1973).

Committee on Consumer Policy, *Labelling and Comparative Testing* (Paris: Organisation for Economic Co-operation and Development, 1972).

Bernard J. McGuire, *Department of Commerce Energy Labelling and Energy Efficiency Programs for Household Appliances* (Springfield, Va.: National Technical Information Service, 1975).

F. A. Paine (ed.) *Packaging and the Law* (London: Newnes-Butterworths, 1973).

Chapter 7

Subject/search headings: marketing, advertising, sales, promotion, competition, restrictive practice, public relations, consumer motivation and behaviour, consumer research, etc.

Christine Hull (compiler), *Principal Sources of Marketing Information* (London: Thomson Organisation, 1977).

Diana Woolley, *Advertising Law Handbook* (London: Business Books, 1976).

National Business Council for Consumer Affairs, Sub-Council on Product Safety, *Guidelines on Advertising Substantiation* (Washington DC: Government Printing Office, 1972).

Paul H. Guenault and J. M. Jackson, *The Control of Monopoly in the United Kingdom* (London: Longmans, 1974).

David Elliot, *Concentration in UK Manufacturing Industry* (London: HMSO, for Department of Trade and Industry, 1974).

G. Walshe, *Recent Trends in Monopoly in Great Britain* (Cambridge: Cambridge University Press for National Institute of Economic and Social Research, 1974).

H. B. Thorelli, H. Becker and J. Engledow, *The Information Seekers: An International Study of Information and Advertising Image* (Cambridge, Mass.: Ballinger, 1975).

E. Dichter, *Consumer Motivations* (1964); H. Stevenson, *Handbook of Public Relations* (1971); V. P. Buell, *Modern Marketing* (1970); R. Barton, *Advertising Management* (1970). (Maidenhead, Berks.: McGraw-Hill).

Periodicals:

MEAL, *Monthly Digest* (Media Expenditure Analysis Ltd, 110 St. Martin's Lane, London WC2).

Campaign and *Marketing* (Haymarket Publishing Ltd, 54–62 Regent Street, London W1A 4YJ).

Journal of Advertising Research (Advertising Research Foundation, 3 E. 54th Street, New York, NY 10022).

Journal of Marketing Research (American Marketing Association, 222 S. Riverside Plaza, Chicago, Ill. 60606).

European Journal of Marketing (MCB European Marketing and Consumer Studies) Ltd, 200 Keighley Road, Bradford, West Yorkshire, BD9 4JZ).

Journal of Consumer Policy (Luchterhand Verlag, Postfach 1780, D-5450 Neuwied 1, West Germany).

ANBAR, *Marketing and Distribution Abstracts* (London: ANBAR/ Institute of Management).

Journal of Consumer Studies and Home Economics (Blackwell Scientific Publications, Osney Mead, Oxford OX2 0EL).

Chapter 8

Subject/search headings: reliability, durability, servicing, spares, obsolescence, life-cycle costs, repair, warranty, guarantee, product liability, etc.

Bureau Européen des Union Des Consommateurs/European Bureau of Consumers' Unions, *After-Sales Service in the European Community* (Brussels: BEUC, 1976).

Center for Policy Alternatives, *Consumer Appliances; the Real Cost* (Springfield, Va.: U.S. National Technical Information Service, 1974).

Center for Policy Alternatives, *Consumer Durables: Warranties, Service Contracts and Alternatives* (Springfield, Va.: U.S. National Technical Information Service, 1974).

Logistics Management Institute, *Life-Cycle Costs: Procurement Cases* (for example, for gas, electric ranges, water heaters, air conditioners, etc.); (Washington DC: U.S. National Bureau of Standards, 1975–7).

Electrical and Television Retailers Association, *Your Electrical and Electronic Products: A Guide to Their Life Servicing and Repair* (London: ETRA, 1976).

Consumer Protection Advisory Committee, *Rights of Consumers: A Report on Practices Relating to the Purported Exclusion of Inalienable Rights of Consumers and Failure to Explain their Existence* (London: HMSO, 1974).

Directorate-General for Internal Market, EEC, *Memorandum on the Approximation of the Laws of Member States relating to Product Liability* (Brussels: Commission of the European Communities, 1974) Ref. Working Document No. X1/332/74-E.

Council of Europe, *Draft European Convention on Products Liability* (Strasbourg: Council of Europe, 1976). Ref. No. DIR/Jur (76) 5.

Consumers' Association, *Product Liability* (London: Consumers' Association (memorandum), 1974).

C. J. Miller and P. A. Lovell, *Product Liability* (London: Butterworths, 1977).

Chapter 9

Subject/search headings: product use, performance, consumer satisfaction, complaints, etc.

Jeremy Mitchell, 'A Systematic Approach to Analysing Consumer Complaints' in *Journal of Consumer Studies and Home Economics* (1977, 1, pp. 3–20).

David Caplovitz, *The Poor Pay More* (New York: Free Press, 1963).

H. Gintis, 'Consumer Behaviour and the Concept of Sovereignty: Explanations of Social Decay' in *American Economic Review* (Papers and Proceedings), 62 (1972), pp. 267–78.

E. K. Hunt and J. G. Schwartz (eds.) *A Critique of Economic Theory* (Harmondsworth: Penguin, 1972).

J. C. Lingoes and M. Pfaff, 'The Index of Consumer Satisfaction: Methodology' in M. Venkatesan (ed.) *Proceedings of the Third Annual Conference of the Association for Consumer Research* (Iowa City: School of Business, Iowa University, 1972), pp. 689–712.

Department of Prices and Consumer Protection, *Consumer Safety* (A Consultative Document) (London: HMSO, 1976).

William G. Johnson, *Product Safety* (London: Industrial and Commercial Techniques Ltd, 1970).

Consumer Index to Product Evaluation and Information Sources (Ann Arbor, Mich.: Pieran Press).

R. L. Heilbroner *et al.*, *In the Name of Profit* (New York: Doubleday, 1972).

J. Martin and G. W. Smith, *The Consumer Interest* (London: Pall Mall Press, 1968).

R. T. Michael, *The Effect of Education on Efficiency in Consumption* (New York: Columbia University Press, National Bureau of Economic Research, Occasional Paper No. 116, 1972).

Don Weller, *Who Buys: A Study of the Consumer* (London: Pitman, 1974).

Susan George, *How the Other Half Dies* (Harmondsworth: Penguin, 1976).

Organisations and institutions

We have listed a few of the many organisations whose work bears on consumer and related issues. Refer to the appropriate directories for detailed information about others.

Apart from national and international general directories, most reference libraries will also stock national guides to major individual organisations or institutions.

There would usually be no more than a three or four line entry in a general directory, such as: *Directory of British Associations, Directory of European Associations* (Beckenham, Kent: CBD Ltd); or *National Trade and Professional Associations of US and Canada (and Labour Unions)* (Washington DC: Columbia Books Inc.). A more specialised directory such as *The Guardian Directory of Pressure Groups* (London: Wilton House) will have more detailed information.

Directories to individual organisations generally identify major departments and senior personnel. These include *The Imperial Calendar and Civil Service List* (central government); *Municipal Yearbook* (local government); *Kompass* (business organisations) among others. When information is not given in a directory or guide, it can often be found in an organisation's annual report or prospectus, or other publication.

Virtually all of the organisations listed below publish (or distribute) material on consumer and related issues—and most will supply details of these, free of charge, on request.

International bodies (government)

Consumer Product Safety Commission, 1111 18th St NW, Washington DC 20207. CPSC publishes many pamphlets and other material on product safety and related subjects. It also maintains the Injury Information Clearinghouse, the Technical Information for Product

Safety Library, and the National Electronic Injury Surveillance System (NEISS).

Commission of the European Communities: Director General of Information, Rue de la Loi 200, B-1049 Brussels (UK office: 20 Kensington Palace Gardens, London W8 4QQ, telephone: 01-727 8090). Economic and Social Committee, 2 Rue Ravenstein, 1000-Brussels. Environment and Consumer Protection Service, 25 Rue Archimede, 1049-Brussels. Numerous publications and periodicals: for example, *Industry and Society, Euroforum*, both of which cover issues related to the subject matter of this book.

National Technical Information Service (US Department of Commerce) is the central source for the public sale of US government-sponsored research reports. Details of weekly abstracts, reports, search facilities, etc. are contained in the NTIS General Catalog *NTIS Information Services*, available free from NTIS at 5285 Port Royal Road, Springfield, Va. 22161.

Organisation for Economic Cooperation and Development, 2 Rue André Pascall, Paris XVI. Several publications by the OECD's Committee on Consumer Policy have been mentioned in the text: many give useful outline information about policies and major developments in OECD member countries.

US Government Printing Office, Washington DC 20204. Publishes *Monthly Catalog* of Government publications with biannual index (available on subscription) and also (free) abstracts of *Selected US Government Publications* of general interest.

Note. Though consumer information in the US is probably more comprehensive, better organised and more accessible than elsewhere, no reference has been made to several US government departments with major responsibilities for consumer affairs (such as Health Education and Welfare, General Services Administration and Federal Trade Commission) in view of the possible reorganisation of departmental responsibilities, following the election of the new administration in 1977. For details, consult the US Government Manual (1977–78 or later) and/or the appropriate departmental directory—both available from the Superintendent of Documents at the Government Printing Office.

International bodies (other)

American Council on Consumer Interests, 238 Stanley Hall, University of Missouri, Columbia, Mo. 65201. Publishers of *Journal of Consumer Affairs*.

Bureau Européen des Unions des Consommateurs (BEUC) 29 Rue Royale, 1000-Brussels. BEUC is predominantly a research organisation, supported by affiliated European consumer organisations. BEUC studies (usually funded by and prepared for the EEC Commission) include reports on Advertising Standards in the UK and Germany (1975); After-Sales Service (1976) and Pharmaceuticals (1978?).

Consumers Consultative Committee to the European Commission (including representative and expert members). See list published in *Euroforum* No. 22/76 (1 June 1976)—Annex 2, p. 1.

Center for Study of Responsive Law, P.O. Box 19367, Washington DC 20036. The Center is the headquarters of Ralph Nader's US organisation (which includes at least a dozen autonomous groups working in specialised fields, such as health research, auto safety, disability rights, corporate accountability and freedom of information). List of major publications (more than forty in paperback, mostly published by Grossman, also by Bantam Books—both New York) available on request. Other publications listed by individual groups.

Consumers' Union, 256 Washington Street, Mount Vernon, New York, NY 10550. Publishers of *Consumer Reports* (the US equivalent of the UK's *Which?*) and other one-off titles. Also: *Consumers' Union News Digest and Product and Industry News*—both abstracts and both available in the UK.

Council on Economic Priorities, 84 5th Avenue, New York, NY 10011. Publishes Newsletter, periodical Reports and one-off studies relating to corporate (consumer, environmental and other) responsibilities. CEP is a non-profit organisation, similar in some respects to Public Interest Research Centre/Social Audit in the UK.

Inform, 25 Broad Street, New York City, NY 10004. A non-profit-making 'social responsibility research group' whose aims and approach are comparable to those of Council on Economic Priorities (q.v.). Publishes a quarterly newsletter and other one-off reports.

Interfaith Committee on Social Responsibility in Investments, Room 846, 475 Riverside Drive, New York City, NY 10027. Publishes *The Corporate Examiner* (monthly newsletter) and other one-off studies relating to business responsibilities—particularly in such areas as racial discrimination and equal employment opportunity and military contracting.

International Organisation of Consumers' Unions, 9 Emmastraat, The Hague, IOCU links many voluntary consumer organisations throughout the world. Publishes *International Consumer* and congress papers and proceedings.

International Institute of Management, Griegstrasse 5, D-1000, Berlin 33. (See publications cited in reading list.)

International Standards Organisation (ISO), 1 Rue de Varembe, 1211-Geneva 20. Publishes *Memento* annually (includes abstracts of internationally agreed standards) and other publications.

UK bodies (government)

For detailed general information on government responsibilities in consumer protection, refer to *Fair Trading and Consumer Protection in Britain* Central Office of Information reference pamphlet No. 144. (This publication also lists thirty-odd official and voluntary bodies concerned with consumer affairs).

Department of Health and Social Security, Alexander Fleming House, London SE1 6BY (telephone 01-407 5522) and Scottish Home and Health Department, New St Andrew's House, St James Centre, Edinburgh EH1 3TF (telephone 031-556 8400). Responsible for food hygiene and safety and licensing of medical products. See HMSO Sectional List No. 11 for publications.

Department of the Environment, 2 Marsham Street, London SW1 (telephone 01-212 3434). Responsible for transport, waste management. prevention of pollution including noise, etc. See HMSO Sectional Lists Nos. 5 and 22 for publications.

Department of Prices and Consumer Protection, 1 Victoria Street, London SW1 (telephone 01-215 7877). Responsible for policy and legislation for most consumer affairs, including monopolies, mergers and restrictive practices, and consumer credit. See Sectional List No. 3. Also publishes *Consumer Information Bulletin*.

Her Majesty's Stationery Office. Retail Bookshop at 49 High Holborn, London WC1 (telephone 01-928 6977) and at Edinburgh, Cardiff, Belfast, Bristol, Manchester and Birmingham (with agents elsewhere). Trade orders, London area and overseas mail-orders, P.O. Box 569, London SE1 9NH. HMSO publishes daily, weekly, monthly and annual lists of government publications, and lists titles by departmental/subject area in Sectional Lists.

Ministry of Agriculture, Fisheries and Food, 3 Whitehall Place, London SW1 (telephone 01-839 7711). Responsible (jointly or otherwise) for safety and quality of food; food labelling and advertising, and use of additives. See Sectional List No. 1.

Office of Fair Trading, Field House, Bream's Buildings, London EC4A 1PR (telephone 01-242 2858). The OFT is responsible to the Secretary of State for Prices and Consumer Protection, and is concerned with the conduct of trade and industry at all levels, and particularly with the administration of monopolies and restrictive practice legislation, the Consumer Credit Act and the Fair Trading Act. OFT publishes a newsletter (*Beeline*) and guides, pamphlets and other material. The booklet, *The Work of the Office of Fair Trading* is available 'to serious students of consumer legislation'.

Price Commission, Neville House, Page Street, London SW1 (telephone 01-222 8020). The Commission was set up under the provisions of the Counter Inflation Act 1973, and has powers to control price increases through administration of the Price Code. The Code applies also to profit margins of manufacturers, service firms and distributors. The Price Commission may also carry out and report on any questions relating to prices, at the invitation of the Secretary for Prices and Consumer Protection. See Sectional List No. 3.

Note. Other government departments with responsibilities for consumer protection include the Home Office (Whitehall, London SW1, telephone 01-213 3000, fire prevention and hazards, see Sectional List No. 26). Department of Trade (1 Victoria Street, London SW1, telephone 01-215 7877, company law and supervision of insurance industry, see Sectional List No. 3); and Northern Ireland Department of Commerce (Chichester House, Chichester Street, Belfast BT1 4JX, telephone 0232-34488. The Department's Consumer Protection Branch has general responsibility for consumer affairs). In addition, the Departments of Energy and Industry have some overlapping responsibilities, see Sectional List No. 3.

For information about local authority trading standards/weights and measures activities, please see *Municipal Yearbook*.

UK bodies (other)

Advertising Standards Authority Ltd, 15/17 Ridgmount Street, London WC1E 7AW (telephone 01-580 0801). Supervises the advertising industry's self-regulatory system for the control of advertising in all non-broadcast media. Publishes: *British Code of Advertising Practice* (5th Edition 1974, as amended) and periodic and annual reports on the working of the control system.

British Institute of Management, Management House, Parker Street, London WC2B 5PT (telephone 01-405 3456). Publishes *Management Review and Digest*, *Management Today*, and many other reports, codes of practice and checklists.

British Standards Institution, 2 Park Street, London W1A 2BS (telephone 01-629 9000). Sponsored by the Department of Prices and Consumer Protection, BSI is 'the recognised body in the UK for the preparation and promulgation of national standards'. Consumer representation on BSI technical committees is arranged through the

Consumer Standards Advisory Committee (formerly the Women's Advisory Committee)—but is extremely modest in relation to representation by industrial/commercial interests. Publications: *Standards, Yearbook, Annual Report, BSI News* and others.

British Safety Council, 62 Chancellor's Road, London W6 9RS (telephone 01-741 1231). Mainly concerned with occupational health and safety, but some activity in transport and product safety as well. Publications: *Safety and Rescue* (monthly tabloid) and other literature.

Consumers' Association, 14 Buckingham Street, London WC2 (telephone 01-839 1222). The UK's major independent consumer organisation. Numerous publications, including *Which?* (and satellite journals on motoring, money, holidays, and do-it-yourself), *Good Food Guide, Drug and Therapeutics Bulletin*, and one-off reports in the Consumer Publications series. (*Speakers' Notes, Daily Consumer News Sheet* and other reports are produced essentially for internal consumption).

Consumer Advice Centres. Information on locations obtainable from Consumers' Association. Enquiries about specific centres should be addressed to the local authority concerned.

Consumer Relations Bureau (J. Walter Thompson Ltd), 40 Berkeley Square, London W1X 6AD (telephone 01-629 9496). Publishes *Consumer Affairs*, bi-monthly, 'to provide advance information on developments in consumer protection, as well as commenting on their likely implications and the response from business'.

Co-operative Union Ltd, Holyoake House, Hanover Street, Manchester M60 0AS (telephone 061-834 0975). Acts as national voice for the UK co-operative movement, and co-ordinates the activities of the different societies and may inform and advise them. Publishes *Co-operative Review* (monthly); *Consumer Code*, and other publications. Refer also to Education Department, Stamford Hall, Loughborough, Leics. LE12 5QR.

Design Council, 28 Haymarket, London SW1Y 4SU (telephone 01-839 8000). Industry-supported body whose aim is to promote good industrial and product design. Publishes *Design* (monthly, ultra-glossy). See also *Booklist*, published annually in the spring.

Friends of the Earth, 9 Poland Street, London W1V 3DG (telephone 01-434 1684). FOE has affiliated local groups, nationwide. Principal concerns are environmental issues, conservation, nuclear safety, etc. Publishes many leaflets and reports including several relating to packaging, reclamation, recycling and reuse. Details on request.

Institute of Purchasing and Supply, 199 Westminster Bridge Road, London SE1 (telephone 01-928 1851)—The national association of purchasing personnel. Publications: *Procurement, Procurement Weekly* (periodicals) and others.

Institute of Trading Standards Administration, Estate House, 319D London Road, Hadleigh, Benfleet, Essex SS7 2BN (telephone 0702 558170). The Institute is the professional organisation of local trading standards officers. Publishes: *Monthly Review* and *Annual Report*.

National Consumer Council, 18 Queen Anne's Gate, London SW1 (telephone 01-930 5752). The NCC (together with associated councils for Scotland, Wales and N. Ireland) is a non-statutory body, financed by government grant (£450 000 in 1976/7). NCC operates as a partisan body, aiming to influence policies which affect consumers through representations, consultation and other means. It has been concerned particularly with problems faced by low-income consumers, and with major issues such as consumer representation in the national-ised industries, and industrial democracy. Publications list available on request.

National Federation of Consumer Groups, 61 Valentine Road, Birmingham B14 7AJ (telephone 021-444 6010). NFCG unites over 50 local voluntary consumer groups in the UK, and on occasion co-ordinates their work. Publishes a newsletter to groups, *Index of Consumer Group Reports* and other occasional publications.

Retail Trading Standards Association 360–66 Oxford Street, London W1N 0BT (telephone 01-629 9314). A conspicuously progressive trade association. Publishes standards of retail practice and other explana-tory guides—details given on request.

Royal Society for the Prevention of Accidents, Cannon House, Priory Queensway, Birmingham B4 6BS (telephone 021-233 2461). Does similar work to British Safety Council (q.v.) but with a greater emphasis on road safety; numerous publications.

Research Institute for Consumer Affairs, Villiers Street, London WC2N 6NE (telephone 01-930 3360). Small independent research unit with charitable status, closely associated with Consumers' Associa-tion (q.v.). RICA has mainly undertaken contract research work into the adequacy of goods and services available for disabled users. Publications: various research reports.

Social Audit Reports 1973-1976

SOCIAL AUDIT 1
The Case for a Social Audit argues for the systematic, independent monitoring of corporate social performance. The report makes a case for direct public and consumer involvement in corporate affairs, and

it looks critically at the role of shareholders who—when it comes to social issues—have taken an unearned income for unassumed responsibilities.

The Social Cost of Advertising examines advertisers' preoccupation with human motivation in buying—rather than with the qualities in a product worth selling. The report scrutinises the voluntary advertising control system and finds serious and widespread weaknesses in it. It argues for a drastic revision of standards and for complete overhaul of the control system.

The Politics of Secrecy is by James Michael, an American lawyer (ex-Nader) and an expert in freedom of information issues. Michael describes his work in Britain in trying to uncover the ultimate secret— the extent of secrecy in government. His report explains how secrecy is calculated to secure political advantage to the consistent disadvantage of Parliament, Press and the public—and it puts the case for a 'public right to know'.

SOCIAL AUDIT 2

Company Law Reform examines the existing, proposed and desirable minimum requirements for the disclosure of information by companies. The report evaluates government proposals for requiring companies to disclose more information, in the light of the government's own record on secrecy—and it identifies some 60 areas in which companies should be required to make public more information about their work.

Arms, Exports and Industry outlines the involvement of some 50 British companies in military contracting, and examines their relationship with the Government Defence Sales Organisation. The report also describes how secrecy has been used to obstruct Parliamentary control over British arms export policies; it concludes that the case for public scrutiny of the 'defence' business, and its effect on the progress of disarmament, is overwhelming.

Something on the Press looks at the way in which several major newspapers recently handled a front-page story. The report describes some of the difficulties reporters face when trying to produce copy to tight deadlines. It describes how, in trying to get round these difficulties, many papers seem to create 'fact' from fiction; make sweeping and unwarranted assumptions about the course of events; mould the story and angle it to what are presumed to be readers' tastes; and then let the news perish, uncorrected and unfinished.

SOCIAL AUDIT 3

Tube Investments Ltd—this is a 30 000 word report on the major UK engineering group, *Tube Investments Ltd*. The report describes the performance of this company under twelve main headings: business operation; company 'philosophy'; disclosure of information; employee relations and conditions of work; minority hiring practices; race relations; health and safety at work; overseas operations; safety, quality and reliability of consumer products; military contracting; environmental responsibilities; and donations to charitable causes.

The report examines the Company's work in each of these areas—so far as was possible without co-operation from the management—and describes what was good, bad or indifferent in each case. The report also discusses some of the general problems and possibilities that might be involved in the assessment of corporate social impact, by means of 'social audits'.

SOCIAL AUDIT 4
Shareholders put to the Test looks at the theory and practice of 'shareholder democracy'. It also describes the response *Social Audit* got from a carefully selected sample of 1000 shareholders in *Tube Investments Ltd*, when trying to table two simple resolutions on social issues, for consideration at the Company's 1974 AGM.
The Unknown Lowson Empire examines a part of the financial empire of Sir Denys Lowson and its impact on a small mining community on the Kentucky/Tennessee border in the USA.

THE ALKALI INSPECTORATE
The Alkali Inspectorate is the government agency responsible for the control of most industrial air pollution. The report on the work of this body examines the way in which it sets and enforces standards and describes the Inspectorate's relationship with local authorities and the public. The 48-page report also examines the confidential relationship between the Inspectorate and industry, and perhaps says as much about the style of government in Britain as it does about the Inspectorate itself.

SOCIAL AUDIT 5
Cable & Wireless Ltd—this report on a publicly-owned corporation —describes the disastrous consequences for the Company of an irregular and unwise involvement in new and unfamiliar business. It explains how, in extricating itself, the Company succeeded in covering up losses amounting to over £2 million. The report also demonstrates how such concealments are facilitated by present auditing and accounting standards.
Advertising: the Art of the Permissible evaluates advertising standards and practice in the light of the attempts made by the industry to strengthen its voluntary control system. The report suggests that the changes that have taken place—though sweeping—remain inadequate to the needs of the present, and certainly to those of the future.

Notes in this issue briefly review seven topics relating to business and government responsibilities.

SOCIAL AUDIT 6

The **Notes** feature reviews at some length industry and government action and inaction on the question of smoking and health. It also follows up with more information on the affairs of the *Cable & Wireless* group, and calls for a public examination of the Company's affairs by the Parliamentary Select Committee on Nationalised Industries. (This Committee subsequently carried out an enquiry into the Company's work.)

Coalite & Chemical Products Ltd is the UK's major producer of domestic solid smokeless fuels. The Company was chosen as the subject of a full Social Audit enquiry both because it plays a key role in the implementation of national clean air policy, and because it carries on operations which are potentially harmful to employees, and which cause serious environmental pollution in the neighbouring communities.

Social Audit's report on *Coalite* runs to some 20 000 words in length and concentrates on an examination of the Company's record in employee relations, health and safety at work, environmental pollution and community and consumer relations.

The report describes how the Company brought badly needed jobs to small mining communities, but at considerable cost to the local environment. It examines in detail the ironical situation whereby households near the plants that manufacture smokeless fuels should be among the last to enjoy the benefits they can bring.

SOCIAL AUDIT 7 and 8 (double issue)

Social Audit on Avon—this issue is devoted entirely to a report on *Avon Rubber Co. Ltd.* This 100 000-word report represents a unique, if not definitive, attempt to describe the major social costs and benefits of financial profitability in one of the largest public companies in the UK.

The investigation of Avon Rubber is the first ever of its kind. It was carried out by *Public Interest Research Centre* on its own initiative and at its own expense—but the research team was given extensive co-operation both by the company's management and by the trade unions concerned. It is believed that no other company in the world has ever agreed to co-operate in such an investigation on these terms.

The *Social Audit* report critically examines Avon's operations under at least 50 different headings. It reveals information which is both a credit to—and damning of—the company. But, above all, the report makes public information about Avon which virtually any other company would insist be kept secret.

However, the significance of the report on Avon goes far beyond the revelation of information about this one company's work. The report not only identifies many 'yardsticks' that might be used in assessing corporate social performance. It also focuses attention on some of the major problems and possibilities for industrial democracy in a traditional but 'progressive' British company.

The report on Avon Rubber was the last in *Social Audit's* journal series of reports. Since mid-1976, reports have been published on an occasional and 'one-off' basis.

Three reports were published between mid-1976 and the end of 1977. All three were reports on contract assignments, highly specialised and of limited general interest.

Social Audit reports due at the time of going to press include: 'Enquiry into the promotion of U.K. food and drug products in Commonwealth Developing Countries' (due Summer 1978); and 'Enquiry into the provision of information to workpeople about toxic substances used at work' (due Spring 1979).

Information about *Social Audit* reports will be given on request. Please send an SAE to Social Audit, 9 Poland Street, London W1V 3DG, England.

Index